Well, Duh!

Our Stupid World and Welcome to It

Bob Fenster

**Andrews McMeel
Publishing**

Kansas City

Library of Congress Cataloging-in-Publication Data

Fenster, Bob.
  Well, duh! : our stupid world and welcome to it / Bob Fenster.
    p. cm.
  ISBN 0-7407-4176-4
  1. Stupidity—History. 2. Stupidity—Anecdotes. I. Title.

BF431.F37 2004
904—dc22   2003063840

04 05 06 07 08 MLT 10 9 8 7 6 5 4 3 2 1

Book design by Lisa Martin
Illustrations by Matt Taylor

This book is dedicated to
everyone who ever thought:
Gee, that was a dumb thing to do.
But not dumb enough.
If I really knuckle down,
I can do something even dumber.

And then they do.

CONTENTS

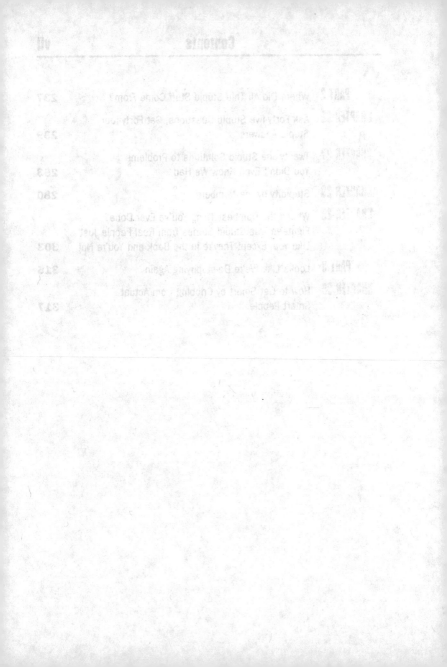

INTRODUCTION

IN 1990 a guy showed up at an Arizona hospital with an unusual problem: He'd been bitten on the tongue while kissing a rattlesnake on the mouth.

But you figure, okay, lesson learned. No one is going to pull that dumb stunt again.

Wrong.

Ten years later, a man in Florida kisses a rattlesnake on the mouth—and gets away with it. So he does it again. And the second time, the snake points out to him why most people don't kiss rattlers.

Why did these men do such a stupid thing? Because they belong to the only species that keeps track of how dumb it is.

But you have to admire the sheer optimism of people willing to push luck that far.

When I wrote my first dumb book, *Duh: The Stupid History of the Human Race*, I figured, okay, that about covers it. From the ancient Europeans who were convinced that trees gave birth to birds to the Detroit burglar who took his dog along on a break-in, people have done just about every dumb thing they can possibly do.

Turns out I wasn't even close.

Stupidity remains an exciting field of opportunity open to everyone. Intelligence has its limitations. Stupidity never says no.

Anytime you think you've seen someone do the dumbest thing you can imagine, keep your eyes open for what's coming next.

Or just start reading this book.

It will make you wonder: If we are all as smart as we think we are, then how can everyone else be as dumb as we think they are?

Being human, we play defense. I may have made some dumb mistakes in my life, but I'm not as stupid as *those* guys.

This book is all about those guys.

PART ONE

23-6: Round-the-Clock Stupidity from People Who Have Trouble Keeping Count

CHAPTER ONE

Egos of the Knuckleheaded: Disinfecting the Common People

CAN YOU really make yourself dumb? Oh yes. It's practically the only way.

But in a world of egotistical Yertles, you might be surprised to find out who wanted to be called His High Mightiness.

Although with competition from spitting llamas and silver dollar–tossing Texans, we might narrow it down by asking: Who is *not* His High Mightiness?

•••

Queen Henrietta of Belgium trained her pet llama to spit—but only at commoners.

3

To prevent assassinations, most royalty treat their personal bodyguards decently. Then there was the nineteenth-century king of Haiti, Henry Christophe, who ordered all his bodyguards to march off a cliff to their deaths. Any guards who refused were executed.

•••

What does a parent with a big ego do when his kid's shelf piles up with soccer trophies, Little League trophies, swim trophies?

According to a woman who runs a California trophy-making business, the proud dad (proud of himself, anyway) orders her to make up some old-looking trophies with his name on them so he can regain household bragging rights.

•••

When eccentric millionaire Ted Turner bought the Atlanta Braves, he experimented with putting their nicknames on the backs of the uniforms. If a player didn't have a nickname, Turner made one up for him.

Pitcher Andy Messersmith was given the nickname Channel. Why? Because his uniform number was seventeen, and channel seventeen was the number of Turner's Atlanta TV station.

•••

Michael Jackson used to visit Disneyland three times a week dressed in wigs, fake beards, hats, and fake noses to blend in with the crowd.

Eventually, Jackson gave up the disguises. Instead, he went to the amusement park in a wheelchair so he could be pushed to the front of the lines and get in first.

•••

James Gordon Bennett, a fussy editor of *The New York Herald*, had some strange newspaper rules. For example, he insisted that all his reporters use the word *night* instead of *evening* because "*night* is a more exact term."

Bennett was finally shown the error of his ways when a reporter filed a story that included a description of a society woman who "looked ravishing in a pink silk night gown."

•••

Calouste Gulbenkian made a vast fortune in the early 1900s through Iraqi oil. He spent his money on European mansions and castles, which he stocked with harems.

He passed the remaining fortune on to his son Nubar, along with this advice for maintaining manageable harems: Get rid of the women after they turn seventeen, when they become impossible to manage.

•••

Nubar Gulbenkian took his father's eccentricities a step further, dressing in Edwardian style throughout the 1950s, wearing top hats, spats, and brocaded jackets to dinner parties.

He also owned a thousand handcrafted canes, which meant he could walk for about three years without having to repeat a cane.

Edith Rockefeller inherited a family fortune, then doubled it by marrying the wealthy Harold McCormick. Edith maintained that she had been an Egyptian queen in a past life—but then who hasn't?

She kept one servant whose sole job it was to convey her orders to the other servants so she wouldn't be obliged to speak to them.

Edith also kept four butlers to serve her personally at mealtime because one or two butlers simply couldn't get the job done right.

•••

Eccentric eighteenth-century British aristocrat Edward Montagu had diamonds sewn all over his clothes. For formal occasions he wore a wig made of iron.

He also had a penchant for getting married indiscriminately. When he died in 1776, he left behind one hundred widows.

•••

The president of Communist Romania, Nicolae Ceauşescu, liked to present himself as a man of the people. This was a tricky business since he also had a phobia of catching germs from other people.

So before Ceauşescu ventured out into the streets to be photographed shaking hands with common people, his secret police would first disinfect the chosen ones.

4 Rulers Who Could Have Given Nicolae Ceauşescu and Donna Summer Ego Lessons

1. As a young boy, Ivan the Terrible, who would become czar of Russia, amused himself by throwing dogs off the roof of the Kremlin.

2. Henry VIII put Thomas à Becket on trial for heresy. Becket didn't take the witness stand in his own defense because he had been dead for 300 years.

3. Zingua, seventeenth-century queen of Angola, kept male concubines. If she really liked one of her love slaves, she had him crippled so he couldn't run away. Zingua felt that such precautionary motivation would make the men better lovers.

4. When Selim I, sultan of Persia, was advised by royal doctors to stop his drinking or he would ruin his health, he ordered the doctors hanged.

   His new doctors made the startling medical discovery that drinking was actually good for the health—theirs.

Donna Summer explained one little-known secret of God's plan: "God had to create disco music so that I could be born and be successful."

•••

If you're fabulously wealthy, what can you do with so much money? Any wacky thing you want.

Millionaire shipping magnate Aristotle Onassis had the bar stools on one of his yachts covered with a unique kind of leather made from the skin of a whale's penis.

•••

Vastly entertaining are the unintended consequences of stupid actions. Michael Romanoff was a con man extraordinaire who so delighted the people he fooled that he eventually ran a successful restaurant in Hollywood, where his pretense of being a Russian prince made his place popular.

Before going into the restaurant business, Romanoff lived the high life by pretending to be rich. In 1931 he impersonated a famous illustrator, Rockwell Kent, which made the artist happy. Romanoff was so winning as Kent that he sold more of Kent's art books than the real artist did.

•••

Polish opera singer Ganna Walska had one of the all-time worst voices in opera. But she had a talent for attracting rich men and getting them to support an almost-career on the stage.

She married millionaire Harold Fowler McCormick, who gave her whatever she wanted: money, houses, jewels, her own opera company. But any time Ganna was scheduled to sing, something would come up to cancel her performance.

In 1920 she was scheduled to open in Chicago but sailed to Europe instead, claiming the company director had insulted her in rehearsal.

McCormick chased after Ganna, promising to buy her a new opera company. Instead, she insisted that her husband have an operation in which monkey glands were implanted in his body to improve his sexual prowess.

He went through with the dangerous operation, and she still threw him out of the mansion.

•••

Texas oilman James Marion West Jr. amused himself by tossing fistfuls of silver dollars around the streets of Houston. He liked to watch people rush after inconsequential money.

West joined the Texas Rangers and designed his own special badge, highlighted with diamonds. He kept ready to take on criminals by toting a .45 in a golden holster and outfitting all his cars with rifles, shotguns, and machine guns.

•••

In the seventeenth century the British elite developed an unusual passion: employing ornamental hermits to live in caves and hollow trees on their estates. The aristocracy felt that quaint mystics injected a proper mood of melancholy into the life of the shire.

Charles Hamilton of Surrey advertised in English news-papers for a prospective hermit. The job requirements:

1. The hermit must never cut hair, beard, or fingernails.
2. He must remain for seven years within the confines of the Hamilton estate.
3. He must never converse with the servants.

If the ornamental hermit lasted under those conditions for seven years, Hamilton would pay him 700 pounds.

The man chosen for the job lasted three weeks.

•••

The Greek leader Herostatus had nothing against the god-dess Diana, yet he burned down her temple at Ephesus in the fourth century B.C. Why? So history would never forget his name.

•••

Everyone knows that billionaire Howard Hughes was a tad eccentric and a hypochondriac of legendary proportions. He refused to discard his urine, saving it to be analyzed for new diseases attacking his body. He saved flakes of his skin for the same reason.

Hughes became convinced that good health could only be maintained by drinking gallons of orange juice, all of which had to be squeezed in his presence. Hughes believed that if the juice was thirty minutes old, it lost all its health-giving qualities.

King Louis XIV of France threw the courtier Francis Seldon into prison, where he remained in solitary confinement for seventy years. Seldon's crime? He'd made a joke about the king being bald.

•••

After he was chosen to be our first president but before the position's title had been decided upon, George Washington suggested that a president should be called His High Mightiness.

Many of the men who have held the position since Washington have also taken that attitude, if not that title.

CHAPTER TWO

Resurrecting the Furniture and Other Dumb Moves in the Face of Fate

STEP 1: Stare fate directly in the eye.

Step 2: Take the flakiest possible disadvantage of your golden opportunity.

Step 3: Welcome to history. You're in.

•••

The paintings of Amedeo Modigliani weren't worth much while he was alive. But after the artist's death, their value shot up.

Many Parisian café owners, who had traded Modigliani drinks for paintings, suddenly were able to cash in.

But one café owner lost a fortune because his wife had scraped the paint off Modigliani's paintings so she could use the canvas to cover beds and sofas.

•••

A Navy mechanic stationed in Spain in 2003 wanted to check the fuel level in a jet fighter, but he didn't have his flashlight. No problem. He simply borrowed a buddy's Bic lighter.

Amazingly, he survived and became a Navy legend.

•••

The Dutch mystic John Roeleveld collected animal bones for forty years, believing the animals that once surrounded the bones would be resurrected on Judgment Day.

He also collected broken furniture and busted machines, believing God would resurrect them too.

•••

Anna Edison Taylor was the first person to go over Niagara Falls in a barrel, a plunge she survived in 1901. What makes her a candidate for legendary stupidity: She couldn't swim. If that barrel hadn't held together, she wouldn't have either.

•••

Buy a few lottery tickets—there's always a chance you'll hit the jackpot. Take a trip to Vegas or Atlantic City—win a little, lose a lot.

But it's not such innocent pleasure when you consider this startling stat: Americans lose over $22 billion each year by gambling.

Someone's getting rich off all that gambling, but it's not the gamblers.

Despite these gargantuan losses, 39 percent of Americans think that buying a lottery ticket is the best way to get rich. And we wonder why telemarketing works.

•••

William Miller, a nineteenth-century preacher, was a convincing prophet. When he declared that the world would end on April 3, 1843, hundreds of his followers killed themselves. They wanted to be the first of the faithful taken up to heaven.

Other Miller converts tried to launch themselves into heaven by running off hills with homemade wings strapped to their backs—making Miller was one of the first preachers to specialize in the spiritual needs of morons.

Despite the repeated failure of these efforts, when Miller announced a new date for the end of the world, July 7, 1843, thousands of his followers who hadn't already killed themselves dug graves and sat in them on that day, waiting for deliverance.

But not before they made Miller rich by purchasing at a special, one-time ascension rate his you-can-take-it-with-you heavenly robes.

An anonymous critic once sent a letter to preacher Henry Ward Beecher. The letter contained a single word: "Fool."

No minister ever received a better setup line, and Beecher made the most of it.

"I have known many an instance of a man writing a letter and forgetting to sign his name," he told his congregation that Sunday. "But this is the only instance I've ever known of a man signing his name and forgetting to write his letter."

•••

When war correspondent and TV newsman Edward R. Murrow was a boy, he bet a friend that he could duck faster than the friend could fire a BB gun. He lost the bet. The pellet hit him between the eyes.

Murrow survived to become one of the most intelligent men on TV, although it's questionable how far TV gets you up the IQ scale.

•••

William Pitt was prime minister of England in the early 1800s. A doctor advised him that drinking a bottle of port each day would maintain his health.

Pitt did the math and reasoned that if he drank six bottles of port a day he would be six times as healthy. He drank himself into the grave at the age of forty-six.

Joseph Gould came from a wealthy family and graduated from Harvard. Then he showed his true mad colors by traveling to North Dakota on a self-inspired research mission to measure the heads of five hundred Mandan Indians and one thousand Chippewas.

After completing his work for the science of physiological irrelevancy, Gould moved to Greenwich Village in the years prior to World War I, where he became the first Bohemian poet.

He once submitted a book review to a small magazine, which wouldn't publish it because the review itself ran two hundred pages long.

Gould became known throughout the Village as Professor Seagull because he would imitate the birds for drinks from tourists. He proclaimed himself the world's leading expert on seagull language.

●●●

John Cleves Symmes was a decorated officer who fought for America in the War of 1812. Then he retired from the military and decided that the earth was hollow.

Symmes tried for years to raise money for an expedition that would enter the hollow earth at the South Pole and emerge at the North Pole.

Other people have postulated a hollow earth, but Symmes's reasoning was particularly interesting: that God would create hollow planets because he was frugal. The Lord would not waste so much matter making solid planets when

He could as easily make planets hollow so people could live in the centers.

Symmes actually found support for his theory in Congress, an institution that has extensive experience with hollowness. Two ships set sail for the South Pole in 1829 to prove his theory correct. They were never heard from again.

●●●

When radios reported the Japanese attack on Pearl Harbor on December 7, 1941, people across the country assumed it was another radio hoax, like Orson Welles's scare of invading Martians. This time they weren't going to be so easily fooled, so they laughed it off.

But it didn't take long for the laughing to stop.

Even when people stateside believed the attack on Pearl Harbor was real, they didn't all have a patriotic reaction. *Life* magazine reported that while the attack was still going on, an Arizona newspaper received a call asking for the score in the football game between the Cardinals and the Chicago Bears.

The caller complained: "Aren't you getting anything besides that war stuff?" No, and not for a long time to come.

●●●

To celebrate the Fourth of July 2001, a man in Kansas City put fireworks in his oven and blew up his kitchen.

He survived the explosion, giving him something to celebrate, but no more fireworks to celebrate with.

Four Curious Final Gestures That Defied the Way the World Usually Works

1. British Army Major Peter Labelliere, who died in 1800, had a clear view of the muddled world. He insisted in his will that he be buried vertically, headfirst. Why?

   "As the world is turned topsy-turvy," Labelliere explained, "it is fit that I should be right at last."

2. Eccentric British philosopher Jeremy Bentham believed that people shouldn't be buried. He recommended that they be mummified, then placed as statues around the garden so children would never lose touch with their ancestors.

   Are you guessing he had this process performed on his own body when he died?

   Dressed in his favorite suit, Bentham was totally varnished, then displayed in a wooden cabinet in University College in London.

3. For some now-forgotten reason, after composer Joseph Haydn died in 1809 his head was separated from his body.

   The severed head was stolen by phrenologists (the bump specialists) who wanted to study the head of a genius.

   Years later, Haydn's head was put on display at the Vienna Academy of Music. But it wasn't until 1954 that someone wondered, what are we doing with the head of a dead composer? What a travesty and sacrilege. Haydn's head was finally returned to be interred with the rest of his remains.

4. In the Philadelphia College of Physicians' Mutter Museum, they keep all kind of strange displays. One of the strangest: a woman who died in 1792 and was buried in earth full of chemicals that turned her body into soap.

The People Who Miss It Entirely Award goes to the *Chicago Times* for complaining about a lousy presidential speech.

The paper ranted: "The cheek of every American must tingle with shame as he reads the silly, flat and dishwatery utterances of the man who has to be pointed out to intelligent foreigners as the President of the United States."

Yes, the *Times* was slamming Abraham Lincoln for his Gettysburg Address.

●●●

The first time Bizet's opera *Carmen* was performed, critics condemned it as obscene. Audiences shunned it. The humiliated composer died three months later.

Now *Carmen* is recognized as a great opera and one of the most popular.

●●●

Actor James Earl Jones was honored with a plaque that was supposed to read: "Thank you, James Earl Jones, for keeping the dream alive." But the engraver made an odd mistake, etching in the name "James Earl Ray" instead. Ray was the man convicted of assassinating Martin Luther King Jr.

Jones said he occasionally gets introduced as James Earl Ray. We have so many famous names in our heads, they trip over each other.

In the 1950s, parents throughout America were worried that their kids would catch polio. When a vaccine was developed, the government set up a program to vaccinate children across the country. But the program quickly ran out of supplies.

Oveta Culp Hobby, the federal official in charge of the program, explained that the government didn't have enough vaccine because "no one could have foreseen the public demand."

No one, that is, except for everyone in the country not working for the federal government.

•••

John Mytton, a nineteenth-century British aristocrat, devised an unusual method of curing his persistent hiccups. He set his clothes on fire. After his servants saved his skin by putting out the fire, Mytton shouted with joy, "The hiccup is gone, by God!"

•••

The German airline Lufthansa offered "nostalgia" rides over London in 2002. The English survivors of World War II could revisit memories by riding in old German bombers, the planes that bombed London during the war.

•••

First, Congressman James Traficant of Ohio was convicted of bribery, tax evasion, and racketeering in 2002. Then he was kicked out of Congress.

Then he really embarrassed himself by threatening TV cameramen: "If you don't get those cameras out of my face, I'm gonna go 8.6 on the Richter scale with gastric emissions that'll clear this room!"

•••

Ines de Castro was crowned queen of Portugal in 1357. Nothing stupid about that. Well, one thing: She was dead at the time of her coronation. But a dead ruler probably gave her subjects less grief than a live one.

•••

Tough-guy actor John Wayne made scores of Westerns, which apparently qualified him to interpret the history of the Old West this way: "I don't feel we did wrong in taking this great country away from them. There were great numbers of people who needed new land, and the Indians were selfishly trying to keep it for themselves."

Wonder if the movie star felt the same way about his own estate.

CHAPTER THREE

Food for Thoughtlessness:
The All-Turnip Diet and Other
Loony Meals at the Mindless Café

WHAT DO you do with a $300,000 bottle of wine? How should you serve flamingo brains? And what's the best dessert to finish off a good meal of Leviticus?

These culinary questions present no problems if you're among the people who don't fire up on all four burners. Here's an extra helping of the incredible eating habits of really weird people.

●●●

When King Mausolus of Turkey died in 353 B.C., his wife had his body cremated. She then mixed his ashes into a glass of wine and drank him.

For odd diets, few people can compare to Menelik II, emperor of Ethiopia in the late 1800s, who ate the Bible for health reasons.

Book eating is an acquired taste. A man from Zanzibar named Dubash Meghji ate an entire Koran. Took him thirty years to do it.

•••

Roman Emperor Elagabalus was a bird brain eater. He preferred flamingo and thrush brains, but was also known to sup on parrot heads.

•••

Some people develop strange eating habits for the good of science.

A California high school teacher in 1993 wanted to demonstrate to his students that what people ate was simply a matter of cultural habit. So he stood up in front of the biology class and ate live mice.

•••

In 1989 a wine merchant proudly held a news conference to display his new acquisition: a 1787 bottle of Chateau Margaux worth $300,000. A minute later it was worth nothing at all—after he dropped the bottle on the floor.

Writer George Bernard Shaw, who was painfully thin, met writer G. K. Chesterton, who was painfully corpulent.

"Looking at you, one would think there was a famine in England," Chesterton pronounced.

"Looking at you," Shaw countered, "one would think you caused it."

●●●

Coming soon to a Japanese restaurant near you: female tables.

In Manchester, England, a Japanese restaurant hoped to start a trend by serving teriyaki, yakitori, and sushi on the bodies of two nude women, who worked as living tables.

"Exquisite food and female beauty combine two essential ingredients that make up the Japanese culture," the restaurant owner explained. Warm those chopsticks, please.

●●●

Coming soon to a Ukrainian restaurant near you: a delicacy invented by a Ukrainian candy company—chocolate-covered pork fat.

Will the treat marketed as Fat in Chocolate catch on in the United States? Or will health-conscious Americans demand the Diet Fat in Chocolate?

●●●

Chickens were first raised for consumption in India five thousand years ago. Until then no one had any idea of what other meat tasted like.

Wine was invented six thousand years ago. Beer has been brewed for four thousand years. So the odds are good that civilization as we know it was first conceived by a couple of guys sitting around drunk one night, and one of them said, "Hey, I've got a crazy idea."

Don't you wonder what our distant ancestors might have come up with if they weren't drunk?

•••

Although opera singer Enrico Caruso depended on good health for his fortune, he ate seven large meals a day, chain-smoked, and consumed garlic, whiskey, and ether to protect his voice.

•••

Horace Fletcher, a nineteenth-century author, wrote influential books on nutrition. He advanced the theory that good health could only be derived if you chewed each bite of food seventy times before swallowing.

You may not be surprised that Fletcher's notions fooled many uneducated people, but he also convinced the famed psychologist William James and the writer Upton Sinclair to sit at table counting their chews.

•••

William Gladstone, prime minister of England for Queen Victoria, didn't fall for such nonsense. He kept his health by chewing every mouthful of food precisely thirty-two times.

Six Cheeses That Sound Too Dumb to Eat

1. Bgug: an Armenian sheep cheese.

2. Bra: a salty Italian cheese.

3. Hay: a French cheese.

4. Leather: a German buttermilk cheese.

5. Potato: a German cheese mixed with mashed potatoes during the processing.

6. Rayon: a Swiss cheese not made of a polyester material.

Oxford professor William Buckland had an extraordinary and universal appetite. Among the things he bragged of dining upon: hedgehog, crocodile, elephant trunk, porpoise head, panther, slugs, earwigs, and dirt.

•••

Actress Ally Sheedy explained the higher consciousness of food in 1987: "If someone's not being a vegetarian, they might be working out some karma, meatwise."

Either that, or they're having dinner.

If health food keeps you healthy, it may eventually lead you to a dilemma described by comedian Redd Foxx when he said, "Health nuts are going to feel stupid someday, lying in hospitals dying of nothing."

●●●

On the other side of the health food debate, almost a million Americans drink Coca-Cola—for breakfast. Soda has no known nutritional value.

●●●

In Arizona there's a roadside restaurant designed to look like the skull of a longhorn steer that died and dried in the desert. You enter through what would have been the cow's nose.

●●●

The poet Lord Byron may have been mad, bad, and dangerous to know, but he was also vain, maintaining a slender figure to attract the ladies he madly pursued.

To keep his looks, the poet's meals consisted of a single potato or, for variety, a small bowl of rice or a few crackers with water.

Not satisfied with starving himself, Byron sweated off more ounces by exercising while wearing seven coats.

Electronics inventor Nikola Tesla was a recluse, living his last years at the Waldorf Astoria Hotel on a diet of crackers and warm milk.

•••

German gourmand Johann Ketzler ate an entire roast ox by himself. Took him forty-two days to do it.

•••

Someone actually measured the steps away that you could hear someone crunch a good pickle. It's ten steps, according to the National Pickle Packers. Things must have been pretty slow down at the Pickle Packers HQ.

•••

An eccentric Englishman ate only one food for the last forty years of his life: turnips.

Or perhaps the all-turnip diet lasted only a couple of weeks and it just felt like forty years.

•••

Throughout history, cooking for royalty has been a risky job, with chefs executed in gruesome fashion when their food displeased the king.

That didn't happen to the chef who cooked for the king of Chantilly. But when a supplier failed to deliver the fish in time for a royal feast, the chef killed himself before the king could get to it.

In 2002 Monsanto announced plans to protect our corn flakes from sogginess by creating a genetically modified crunchy corn flake. How? By injecting a waxy gene into a strain of supercorn.

While they're at it, maybe they could inject a gene that makes dried cereal not stick to the bowl when your kids don't clean up after themselves.

●●●

Sir Tatton Sykes forbade the tenant farmers on his English estate to grow any flowers, commanding: "If you wish to grow flowers, grow cauliflowers."

●●●

Irish writer Jonathan Swift *(Gulliver's Travels)* had an ambulatory dining peculiarity. He took all his meals while pacing around his house, as a way of losing weight while eating.

●●●

While on the campaign trail in Springfield, Illinois, Richard Nixon ate only one bite of a buffalo burger. A Nixon fan scooped up the rest of the burger and kept it as a souvenir.

●●●

Think we've got too much government now? During the reign of Queen Elizabeth I in England, the government ordered people to eat fish three days a week because the fishing industry needed the money.

The English also passed a law that prohibited anyone from drinking in taverns late at night—unless they were spies. Must have been rather tricky for thirsty spies to maintain their cover.

•••

We blame the English for English muffins. But they're innocent, at least of this charge. They were American creations, for which we didn't want to take the credit. Let's own up: American muffins, at last the truth can be told.

•••

If Madame Rosa were really psychic, she could make a fortune by opening the Psychic Café. No reservations needed. We knew you were coming, and we have your favorite table ready. No menus either. Here's the food you had in mind, and thanks in advance for such a generous tip.

CHAPTER FOUR

Finding Enough Flashlights for the Turtles: The Flamboyant Numskullery of Artists and Writers

BENJAMIN Haydon was a nineteenth-century British artist. Or so he thought.

But critics scorned him. Collectors ignored him. Art lovers rejected all his efforts at painting. Despondent over his failures to establish himself as an artist, Haydon killed himself.

After his death, Haydon's journal was published as an autobiography. The book proved to be a hit, popular with critics and readers alike. Haydon wasn't an artist after all; he was a writer—only he never knew it.

This is why the only people who become writers and artists are the people who have to.

The free-spirited American poet Maxwell Bodenheim challenged the eccentric writer Ben Hecht to a formal debate in front of the Dill Pickle Club to determine whether the people who attend literary debates were imbeciles.

Hecht marched to the stage, looked over the audience, and declared, "The affirmative rests."

Bodenheim countered by gazing around the auditorium, then turning to Hecht and declaring, "You win!"

●●●

Artist Robert Rauschenberg once staged a work of performance art in which thirty large turtles were set loose on stage with flashlights strapped to their shells.

Around the turtles, an actor danced with tin cans on his knees. Another actor ripped up a phone book, while three actresses in bridal gowns walked through the audience handing out crackers.

●●●

Louis Stone was an inventive newspaper reporter in the 1890s working for the *Evening Citizen* of Winstead, Connecticut. He turned away from producing the typical boring newspaper story and wrote whoppers instead. But readers liked the stories even when they found out they weren't true.

Instead of being fired by a self-righteous editor, Stone became famous as the Winstead Liar, writing accounts of a cat that could whistle "Yankee Doodle," a tree that grew baked apples, a hen that laid red, white, and blue eggs on the Fourth of July, and a man who painted a spider web on his bald head to keep flies away.

•••

George VI of England didn't know much about art, but then he didn't know much about anything else either.

When the king attended an art exhibit, he commented to a painter who specialized in storm scenes, "Pity you had such bloody awful weather."

•••

Nobody trashes a writer like another writer. Here's Gore Vidal, on Aleksandr Solzhenitsyn: "He is a bad novelist and a fool. The combination usually makes for great popularity in the U.S."

•••

You haven't arrived until you're a crop circle artist. Bulgarian artist Daniel Bozhkov turned a Maine hayfield into a crop-circle portrait of TV talk show host Larry King by flattening a field of timothy and milkweed into an artwork entitled *Learn How to Fly Over a Very Large Larry*.

•••

The half-mad English poet Lord Byron believed the fortune teller who predicted he would die at thirty-seven.

So if you're already a little off and think you won't survive anyway, might you not be tempted to fulfill that prophesy by living wildly toward death? Especially if you were a poet?

Perhaps a more reasoned attempt to survive would have

led Byron to a long life. Or maybe not. The poet died at thirty-six. So had his father. So did his daughter Augusta.

●●●

Is the cemetery the place where the stupid and the bizarre meet? Poet of the macabre Edgar Allan Poe was buried in a pauper's plot in 1850. Twenty-five years later, fans of his dark verse reburied Poe in an honored grave.

But before they reinterred the poet, they broke off pieces of Poe's rotted coffin and took them home for souvenirs, a debased denouement Poe might have written himself.

●●●

In 1989 Colonel Muammar el-Qaddafi, ruler of Libya, informed the world that Shakespeare was not English. He was an Arab.

●●●

Painter Marcel Duchamp gave several of his paintings to the artistically revolutionary bata movement. They chopped the paintings to pieces with axes—as artists, not critics.

●●●

We all have that picture in our minds of the starving artist in the freezing garret struggling against poverty to produce great, unappreciated art.

Then there's the artist Christo, whose *Running Fence*, a 1968 installation along the coast of Northern California, was built from 2,050 steel posts, 165,000 yards of cloth, and $2,250,000 in support funding.

British poet Matthew Arnold toured the United States giving a series of readings, including one attended by General Ulysses S. Grant.

But the poet spoke so softly that no one in the audience could hear his poems. When he refused to speak up, people left. Arnold kept whispering his poetry to empty halls.

•••

English playwright George Bernard Shaw was not fond of America, so he was an odd choice to be given the honor of making the first transatlantic phone call. Shaw's historic greeting: "Hello, America, how are all you boobs?"

•••

When George Bernard Shaw toured the United States in 1933, he gave numerous newspaper interviews, during which he advised that the only hope for America was to get rid of the Constitution.

•••

PR flack Harry Reichenbach proved the power of public relations when he hired people to stare in the window of an art gallery at an unknown painting of a nude woman called *September Morn*.

When the publicity led to the arrest of the artist and gallery owner for indecency, the painting became famous and millions of prints were sold.

Three Cases of Stupid Inspiration

1. Writer Hart Crane found poetic inspiration by insulting everyone, getting into fistfights, breaking tables and chairs, then listening to *Bolero* by Ravel.

2. Painter Salvador Dalí grew a long mustache, then waxed it into pointed ends and turned them up, declaring the tips to be inspirational antennas.

   "My mustache is my radar," the artist explained. "It pulls ideas out of space."

3. The nineteenth-century French poet Ferdinand Flocon drew his inspiration from the laws of France. He devoted his life to turning the entire French Civil Code into an epic poem.

The wealthy poet Tristan Tzara and his eccentric friend, the artist Hans Arp, created the absurdist Dada "movement against all movements."

They chose the movement's name blindly out of a French dictionary by stabbing the book with a penknife. The knife landed on the word *dada*, which meant hobbyhorse.

During performances, the Dada artists antagonized people with nonentertainment, and the audience enthusiastically joined in by throwing unusual objects at the performers.

This led one Dadaist to shout at the audience, "You are all idiots," which apparently qualified them to be presidents of the Dadaist movement.

•••

Dr. Albert Barnes, a millionaire drug manufacturer, owned a vast collection of paintings by Matisse, Renoir, Cézanne, and Picasso. But he refused to let other collectors, art scholars, or art lovers see the paintings.

The only visitors he allowed to view his vast collection of modern art were people who had no interest in it. It was his way of showing the world that the art belonged to him, not to humanity.

•••

e.e. cummings, the poet who eschewed capital letters, was thrown into prison in France for felony grammar.

French authorities suspected that his eccentric poetry contained some kind of spy code. The poet made good use of the time he spent locked in a prison cell by writing a book, *The Enormous Room*.

English artist Catherine Gregory protested animal abuse by exhibiting mangled animals in an art gallery, including a dog and rabbits cut into pieces, and sixty-three mice flattened and mounted as sculpture.

•••

The art of mutilated animals was also practiced by Christian Lemmerz, a Danish artist whose 1994 exhibit consisted of six pigs decomposing under glass.

•••

Sherlock Holmes was the smartest detective in literature. But Sir Arthur Conan Doyle, who wrote the books, had a little trouble with the elementary facts.

In *A Study in Scarlet*, Doyle mentions that Dr. Watson was wounded in the shoulder during the war. But in *The Sign of the Four*, the bullet wound has migrated to Watson's leg.

•••

What happens when talented writers go Hollywood? They sacrifice their art and make enough money to sit around the pool all day and complain about it.

"I'm a Hollywood writer," playwright Ben Hecht moaned, "so I put on a sports jacket and take off my brain."

•••

Cartoonist Jules Feiffer nailed the attraction of the artistic life. "Artists can color the sky red because they know it's blue," he explained. "Those of us who aren't artists must color things the way they really are or people might think we're stupid."

●●●

"One reason the human race has such a low opinion of itself is that it gets so much of its wisdom from writers," writer Wilfrid Sheed said.

●●●

The next time you're visiting a museum and overhear someone pontificating about the meaning of art, remember this bit of wisdom from art lover Edmond de Goncourt: "A painting in a museum hears more ridiculous opinions than anything else in the world."

●●●

George S. Kaufman explained that he preferred to write one-liners for comedian Milton Berle instead of Broadway plays because writing jokes "doesn't tire my hair."

●●●

Here's the answer writers have been looking for to throw back at editors who criticize the grammatical errors in their work.

The perfect response was offered by nineteenth-century English poet Alfred Austin, who parried an editor's attack with this reasonable defense: "I dare not alter these things. They come to me from above."

Any readers who find typos not to their liking in this book, please see above.

CHAPTER FIVE

Thirteen-Cent Bail
and the Missing Sponge:
The Surprising Numskullery
of Doctors and Lawyers

WHAT'S the difference between God and a lawyer? God doesn't think he's a lawyer.

Now, what's the difference between God and a doctor? The doctor doesn't think God's a doctor.

●●●

In North Carolina a surgeon was operating for an aneurysm in 1994 when he stopped in the middle of the procedure to go to lunch. He left the anesthetized patient alone on the operating table while he and the nurses chowed down.

In 1971 a Pennsylvania attorney brought a lawsuit against the devil. But it was thrown out of court because the judge ruled that Satan was not a Pennsylvania resident.

•••

We've all heard those urban legends about a surgeon who stupidly left a clamp or sponge inside a patient's body, then sutured up the incision.

It's such a wild story—hardly ever happens. Wrong. A 2003 study published in the *New England Journal of Medicine* found that it happens on an average of 1,500 times a year. Hopefully not by the same surgeon.

•••

In 1979 a man sued the Coors beer company for turning him into an alcoholic. He claimed that Coors beer didn't have a label on the can warning drinkers that it contained alcohol.

•••

A Pakistani who wasn't a doctor convinced English authorities that he was in 1992 and obtained a medical license. Before he was stopped, he prescribed that patients drink shampoo, take sleeping pills every six hours, or swallow suppositories.

•••

Nebraska Judge Richard "Deacon" Jones once set bail for a defendant at thirteen cents. Another time he declared bail to be "a zillion pengos," which was hard for the defendant to meet since the judge never told anyone what a pengo was.

But that's to be expected from a judge who sometimes signed court documents as "Snow White."

•••

Doctor, inject thyself. John Hunter, the leading English surgeon of the eighteenth century, injected himself with venereal diseases to study the effect. The effect was that syphilis killed him.

•••

A Dutch doctor, Bart Huges, wanted to experiment with trepanation, the medieval practice of drilling holes in a patient's head to cure various ailments. Huges thought it would help him achieve a permanent and drugless high.

When he couldn't find a doctor to perform the procedure, Huges took an electric drill and bored a hole in his own head in 1965. He survived the operation, which led to a brief flurry of experimentation with self-trepanation, particularly in Great Britain.

•••

In Texas Judge Charles Hearn signed a death warrant by adding a smiley face to his signature. In a 1993 appeal, the defense lawyer argued that it was like the judge saying, "have a nice death."

Eleven Dumb Cures

1. If anyone in the court of Russia's Ivan the Terrible complained about a headache, the czar had his soldiers cure it by pounding nails into the person's head.

   Didn't stop the headaches. Did stop the complaining.

2. As the bubonic plague spread across Europe during the Middle Ages, so did stupid treatments for the disease, including medicines made from pulverized emeralds and melted gold.

   The patient may not have lasted long, but he did feel like a million bucks before he died.

3. A second popular treatment for the plague: spreading lard into the open wounds caused by the disease.

4. In the 1600s doctors came up with an ironic attempt to prevent the plague. They advised patients to smoke tobacco for their health.

5. But that's nothing compared with the cure devised for malaria in the thirteenth century: taking splinters from gallows where the English hung criminals and rubbing the sick person with them.

6. For stomach ailments, doctors in the Middle Ages recommended cleansing the digestive tract with a glass of water and millipedes twice a day.

7. In 2003 a psychic healer became popular in Lithuania by taking toilet paper that was energized by God and wrapping it around sick people to cure their illnesses. Why God would choose to bless toilet paper was not made clear.

8. Europeans once believed that you could cure syphilis by having sex with a virgin.

9. Russians believed that if you hid a piece of pork in the bed of a Jewish person for nine days, then ate it, you could cure your addiction to alcohol.

10. In ancient Greece, people believed you could catch leprosy by drinking beer. On the other hand, they believed that epilepsy could be cured with flute music.

11. In the 1600s people throughout Italy and France were seized by a poison panic, convinced they were slowly being murdered with an invisible poison that had no taste, odor, or color.

    These people thought the only way to protect themselves against the poison was to hold public executions of everyone in their city jails, no matter what their offense, even if they'd not been convicted of anything.

Have you heard the one about the doctor . . . Dana Carvey, the funniest TV comedian to have a generally dull movie career, was put out of commission for several years as he recovered from a botched double-bypass operation in which his doctor cut on the wrong artery.

●●●

In 3000 B.C. a Babylonian law decreed that a doctor could have his hands cut off if his patient died—unless his patient was a slave, in which case he merely owed the slave owner another slave.

The unintended side effect of this law was to reduce the number of doctors willing to treat anyone but slaves.

●●●

In the early 1900s, Dr. Albert Abrams claimed to have invented a medical tool that could diagnose patients over the telephone. He also claimed he could tell what was wrong with a person by examining his handwriting without ever seeing the patient.

Abrams invented many mysterious medical devices, all of which had the capability to separate gullible patients from their money.

●●●

A Pennsylvania judge was tossed off the bench in 1992 for offering to reduce sentences if defendants let him shampoo their hair. Was there no justice for bald criminals?

Eight Great Dumb
Moments in Legal History

All lawyers can't be Perry Mason, but here are some amazingly witless cross-examinations from actual court cases:

1. "Were you alone or by yourself?"

2. "Now doctor, isn't it true that when a person dies in his sleep, he doesn't know about it until the next morning?"

3. "You were there until the time you left, is that true?"

4. "How far apart were the vehicles at the time of the collision?"

5. "How many times have you committed suicide?"

6. Q: "So the date of conception (of the baby) was August 8th?"

   A: "Yes."

   Q: "And what were you doing at that time?"

7. "The youngest son, the twenty-year-old, how old is he?"

8. "Were you present when your picture was taken?"

If you were going to become a medical quack, you should have done it in England during the 1700s. Such remedies as these were popular among the ill (or people who became ill once they took the cures): elk hooves, crab claws (black tips only), live toads, burned coke, live hog lice, skin of a capon's gizzard, pike jaw, newly gathered earthworms, and dried dung (peacock or goose).

●●●

The ancient Greek scholar Pliny developed a fascination with dentistry, although few of his patients shared his interest.

According to Pliny, you could avoid toothaches simply by eating a couple of mice every month.

To get rid of bad breath, he prescribed a combination of toads, frogs, ox, and worms. History does not record how bad the breath was that such a mixture improved.

●●●

In the early 1900s a group of English doctors became convinced that the colon was the cause of numerous diseases. So hundreds of patients had their colons removed as a treatment for diseases that had nothing to do with the colon.

●●●

Russian Premier Vladimir Putin sued the makers of the Harry Potter films for misappropriating his face.

The leader of all Russia felt that Hollywood's SFX guys had digitized his face to create the computer-generated Dobby the house-elf for *Harry Potter and the Chamber of Secrets*. Not only does Putin have a good face for an elf, he's got a great elf name: Putin the house elf.

•••

Dr. Walter Freeman developed a quick method of giving patients lobotomies using an ice pick and a hammer. He toured the country in the 1950s in an operating van he called the Lobotomobile, and convinced doctors and patients to let him perform 20,000 of these crude, on-the-spot operations.

•••

English doctors in the eighteenth century developed a unique method of extracting diseased teeth. They looped catgut around the offending tooth, tied the other end of the string to a bullet with a hole drilled in it, then fired the bullet (and the tooth) from a revolver.

•••

A Hungarian doctor, Ignaz Semmelweis, shocked the medical world in the 1850s by suggesting that doctors could protect their patients from infections simply by washing their hands.

This theory was so offensive to the European medical establishment that Semmelweis was forced out of his hospital post.

CHAPTER SIX

Hollyweird:
Birdbrains in Tinseltown

YOU DON'T have to be a dumbbell to become a Hollywood celebrity. But it certainly can't hurt your chances.

To understand Hollywood, it helps to remember the basic idiotic rule of movies: If you have a movie script with two real ideas in it, what you really have is a hit and a sequel.

•••

When director Cecil B. DeMille made his epic *The Crusades*, he was having trouble getting the right performance from one of the stars, Loretta Young.

David Niven reported that Young read one of her key lines

as, "Richard, you gotta save Christianity." When the director suggested she put more awe into the line reading, she changed it to: "Aw, Richard, you gotta save Christianity."

•••

The dumb Hollywood scorecard: The movie *Dumb and Dumber* was ten times as popular as *Sense and Sensibility* and a thousand times more popular than *The Search for Signs of Intelligent Life in the Universe.*

•••

Movie star Mary Astor claimed that fellow star Joan Crawford was on a movie set on December 7, 1941, when someone rushed into the sound stage to announce that the Japanese had "destroyed Pearl Harbor."

"Oh dear," Joan said, "who was she?"

•••

Party Harvey: At Jimmy Stewart's bachelor party at Chasen's restaurant, the entertainment was provided by midgets dressed in diapers.

•••

Many people who work in showbiz think the Oscars are a joke, despite the pomp and pretense of the annual ceremony.

As actor Vic Morrow put it: "Are we honestly supposed to believe that the Academy Awards are for acting ability when John Wayne has won the Oscar but Richard Burton hasn't?"

Ten Hollywood Insiders Who Say Other Hollywood Stars Are Not the Shiniest Coin in the Purse

1. Comedian Totie Fields: "Goldie Hawn is as bright as a dim bulb."

2. French actress Anouk Aimee: "Warren Beatty is like a masculine dumb blonde."

3. Filmmaker Andy Warhol: "Mickey Rourke is just so adorable. Dumb, but with some magic."

4. Pop singer Boy George: "Andy Warhol is an idiot, like a big cheesecake on legs."

5. Movie director Tony Richardson about actress Vanessa Redgrave: "A great actress, not a great thinker. Me, I'm leftist. Her, she's often just plain lunatic."

6. Filmmaker Otto Preminger: "Directing Marilyn Monroe was like directing Lassie. You needed fourteen takes to get one right."

7. Actress Constance Bennett jumping on the Marilyn Monroe bimbo wagon: "There's a broad with her future behind her."

8. Critic John Simon about actress Sandy Dennis: "She balanced her postnasal condition with something like a prefrontal lobotomy, so that when she is not a walking catarrh, she is a blithering imbecile."

9. Director Derek Jarman about actors Melanie Griffith and Don Johnson, who were married to each other at the time: "She couldn't play smart to save her life. Being a dumb blonde must run in that family."

10. And if you think the stars are less than bright, listen to actor John Carradine: "The worst jerks in this business are the directors who think they can write. Directors can't do anything but direct. Otherwise, they wouldn't be directors."

Actor James Coco observed that aging star Don Ameche won an Oscar for "break-dancing in *Cocoon*. Only all his dancing was done by a stunt double. Doesn't the dancer deserve his own junior Oscar?"

It cost Hollywood $100 million to make the movie *Titanic*. It cost the ship builders $3 million to build the *Titanic*.

•••

Director Alfred Hitchcock's granddaughter asked for his help writing a school paper analyzing one of his films, *Shadow of a Doubt*. When the girl turned in the paper, they got a C.

•••

The producers of *All the President's Men*, the movie about the *Washington Post* reporters who exposed Nixon's Watergate scandal, grew obsessive about authenticity. They actually flew trash from the real newspaper out to Hollywood to play the newsroom trash in the movie.

•••

In Hollywood they just call this normal: Movie star Fattie Arbuckle owned a car with a built-in toilet. To amuse guests, he once staged a fancy wedding between two dogs.

•••

Here's a rare Hollywood case of reverse ego. "There are not many things that make me laugh," comedian Chevy Chase admitted, "and that includes me."

•••

Movie stars can be just as dumb as regular people. But no one will tell them they don't have a lick of sense because celebrities have what even smart people desire: a license to do whatever they want.

Silent movie star Charlie Chaplin became so big in Hollywood and his own mind that he not only starred in movies, he insisted upon starring at every party he went to.

Chaplin actually negotiated with the hosts for the right to be the first guest to arrive at Tinseltown parties.

●●●

Erich von Stroheim, the eccentric Austrian film maker, set the standard for Hollywood excess in the 1920s by spending a studio fortune on sets and authentic props.

The director explained why he went over budget to outfit a film regiment with real Imperial Guard silk underwear. "The public, of course, will not see the underwear," von Stroheim explained. "But the actors must know they are wearing authentic Prussian undergarments."

●●●

Hollywood makes expensive epics for one reason, and movie producer Joe Levine knew it when he said, "You can fool all the people all the time if the budget is big enough."

●●●

Back in 1952 when deepies (or 3-D movies) first came out, critics predicted no one would go along with wearing special 3-D glasses to see a movie.

But they did. As Paramount exec Bill Thomas pointed out, "They'll wear toilet seats around their necks if you give 'em what they want to see."

Toilet Seats: The Movie—I can see it now.

●●●

In 1988 religious protestors were offended by the film, *The Last Temptation of Christ*. To picket the studio that produced the film, the protestors drove out to Universal Studios, which made $4,500 off them in parking charges.

●●●

Hollywood knows great movies *after* they become hits—but not before.

The entire movie industry loved these two films once they scored big. But the scripts for both movies had gone begging all over Hollywood, with no studios wanting to make the films.

Forrest Gump was turned down for nine years. *One Flew Over the Cuckoo's Nest* was rejected for fifteen years.

Both of them won Oscars for Best Picture.

●●●

Movie stars Errol Flynn and John Barrymore, great friends, were both heavy drinkers. When Barrymore died, his Hollywood cronies stole his body and snuck it into Flynn's house, where they propped the actor up in a chair with a drink in his hand and a cigarette between his lips.

When Flynn entered the room, he was so shocked he took a vow of abstinence on the spot.

Movie studio boss Samuel Goldwyn said the wackiest things, inventing the category of one-liners so dumb, they're smart. Consider:

"I had a monumental idea this morning, but I didn't like it."

"The trouble with directors is they're always biting the hand that lays the golden egg."

"I read part of it all the way through."

"Let's bring it up to date with some snappy nineteenth-century dialogue."

"The publicity for this picture is sweeping the country like wildflowers."

"You've got to take the bull between your teeth."

●●●

You don't have to look far to find stupidity in Hollywood. But it's worth a trip back to the dumb days of the 1950s, when they matched some of the silliest movies ever made with some of the silliest movie promotions.

Here's how they tried to shock audiences with B-movie schlock (and oh, how quaint it all looks now):

High School Hellcats—"The facts about the taboo sororities that give them what they want!"

The Cat Girl—"Screaming terror. To caress me is to tempt death."

Alimony—"Alimony racketeers prey on innocent dupes!"

The Unholy Wife—"Half angel, half devil, she made him half a man."

Blonde Ice—"Beautiful, evil, bedeviling, daring!"

Blonde Bait—"The kind of mistake a man can only make once." (Have you ever seen a mistake a man can only make once? Usually takes him three or four times just to get rolling.)

Teenagers from Outer Space—"Teenage hoodlums from another world on a horrendous ray-gun rampage!"

Teenage Caveman—"Prehistoric rebels against prehistoric monsters."

Youth Runs Wild—"It explodes in your face!"

I Was a Teenage Frankenstein—"Body of a boy, mind of a monster, soul of an unearthly thing!"

Girls in Prison—"The shocking story of one man against a thousand women."

You just can't find movies this ridiculous anymore. That's what television is for.

CHAPTER SEVEN

On the Home Front:
Faint-Not Jones and the Family
That Never Said No

AMERICANS spend eight months of their lives opening junk mail. So is it any surprise that on average Americans are in a bad mood 110 days of the year?

One more statistic from the home front: 80 percent of all the morons in the world are in families like these:

•••

James Vincent Forrestal, secretary of defense after World War II, was the early model for Workaholic of the Future.

He was working in London when he received a phone call from his two sons, who had missed their plane in Paris.

Forrestal told the boys to work out the problem themselves and meet him in London.

His sons were ages six and eight at the time.

●●●

Music was an essential part of utilitarianism, the philosophy dreamed up by Jeremy Bentham in the 1700s.

To surround himself with music all the time, he kept a piano in each room of his house (yes, including the bathroom). Then he hired musicians to play all those pianos day and night.

●●●

In 1990 Imelda Marcos threw a birthday party for her husband, the Filipino dictator Ferdinand—who was dead at the time but attended anyway, inside a refrigerated casket.

●●●

In 1990 a man in Clayton County, Georgia, discovered that his wife had committed suicide. But before he called the police, he realized that he shouldn't make a bad situation worse. So he sat down to watch the rest of the Super Bowl, then called.

●●●

In nineteenth-century England, John Fransham ran for Parliament on a platform of outlawing the making of beds more than once a week on the grounds that it was too effeminate.

Three Things Famous People Said That Defy You to Explain Them to Your Kids

1. "We've got to pause and ask ourselves: How much clean air do we need?"

    —Auto manufacturer Lee Iacocca

2. "Hawaii is a unique state. It is a small state. It is a state that is by itself. It is different from the other forty-nine states. Well, all states are different, but it's got a particularly unique situation."

    —Vice President Dan Quayle

3. "Life is very important to Americans."

    —U.S. Senator Bob Dole

Writer Bill Vaughn pointed out the essential stupidity of suburban sprawl: "Suburbia is where the developer bulldozes out the trees, then names the streets after them."

In 2003 a father in Scotts Valley, California, was arrested for leaving his toddler alone in an SUV for forty-five minutes in a mall parking lot. What was Dad doing while baby was waiting in the car seat? Sitting in a restaurant taking part in a Bible study group.

Maybe they were studying family values, you think?

•••

Martin Luther, the great religious reformer of the sixteenth century, was determined to liberate people from the abuses of the church. Yet when Luther turned his brilliant, religious mind to the plight of women, he dismissed them by saying, "Let them bear children till they die of it. That is what they are for."

•••

Think people give their kids crazy names today? In the sixteenth century, English Puritans named their children such instructive names as Love-God Smith, Live-Well Johnson, Faint-Not Jones, Accepted Morgan, and Fight-the-Good-Fight Wellington.

•••

Carry Nation led the fight against alcohol and for Prohibition. But she was just as tough on her husband as she was on saloon owners.

Nation's husband was a preacher, but apparently not a good one. So his wife would sit in the front pew and correct him as he preached.

Or she would stand up in the middle of a sermon and lead the congregation out of the church, announcing that he'd said "quite enough for today." Rev. David Nation was left preaching to an empty church because no one wanted to cross his wife.

●●●

John Humphrey Noyes, who graduated from Yale Divinity School, created his own church around ideas that would be advanced in our own time. But Noyes started his free love church in 1835.

His Putney Corporation of Perfectionists owned everything communally and practiced multiple partners. Noyes preached that fidelity in marriage was a "sin of selfishness" and that his congregation had to "love all other members equally," which meant that no one should ever say no to anyone else.

The community thrived for twenty-five years before falling apart from jealous divisions.

Another of Noyes's unusual notions was that parental love was to be discouraged as idolatrous, so that all children were taken from their birth parents and raised by foster parents.

●●●

When Charles II was king of England, he realized there was one greater protection against usurpation than bodyguards—his brother James.

James was so unpopular that Charles told him, "No one is going to assassinate me in order to make you king."

Should divorced fathers pay child support? Consider the Italian court in 2002 that ordered a father to pay $700 a month in child support.

What's wrong with that? The son was thirty years old and made a good living on the stock market. But the court ruled against the father because his son was a *mammoni,* a mama's boy.

●●●

Louis XI, king of France, was out riding in a forest when a courtier brought him the news that his baby son had died. The king had the forest burned to the ground.

●●●

Novelist John O'Hara was a heavy drinker and a prankster. During Prohibition, he'd dump his empty gin bottles on the porches of neighbors who led the town's anti-liquor campaign.

●●●

Before North Carolina became the progressive, liberal state it is today, public libraries required parental permission before children could check out such risqué reading material as the Bible.

●●●

Sir Walter Raleigh got into a dispute with his son while both were at a dinner party. The enraged father struck his son, but the young Raleigh was too polite to strike back.

Instead, he turned and hit the man sitting on the other side of him, then told him, "Box about. It will come to my father anon."

The idea of everyone hitting everyone else in line struck the fancy of the British elite as an apt metaphor for the Elizabethan Age, and "box about" became a popular saying.

●●●

Lady Hester Stanhope was an eccentric nineteenth-century British aristocrat. She lived her final years in an Arabian monastery, whose rooms she sealed to thwart thieves.

After Lady Hester died, the rooms were opened—to reveal that they contained nothing but rubbish. But at least no one had stolen any of it.

●●●

Hollywood is big on excess. When child star Shirley Temple turned eight, she received 135,000 presents.

By the time the kid could play and wear that many gifts, she'd be too old for them. But can you imagine the thank-you notes Shirley's publicist had to write?

●●●

In 2002 the Bush administration issued a report that found the silver lining in global warming—it could lower your home fuel bills.

I doubt it. If they make the planet so warm that we could turn down the heat in January, the government would just add on a surcharge for insufficient furnace usage.

On a closing note, here's one from my personal home file: No matter how smart you think you are, your four-year-old knows better.

When my son Teddy was four, he was telling me about his friend Casey, who has five brothers and sisters. "Is Casey the oldest in the family?" I asked him.

"No," Teddy explained, "his dad and mom are the oldest."

CHAPTER EIGHT

Dumb in School:
Vertical Thinking and
the Aboriginal IQ Test

"MEN ARE born ignorant, not stupid," philosopher Bertrand Russell said. "They are made stupid by education."

Here are the people who got an A for effort:

•••

When Harvard president Charles Eliot was congratulated for helping to make the university a storehouse of knowledge, he said, "I scarcely deserve credit for that. It is simply that the freshmen bring so much and the seniors take away so little."

In 2000 the University of Wisconsin published a brochure to attract students to the college. To show that UW supported diversity, the school digitally added a black student to the cover photo by pasting in his image using a computer program.

●●●

Prime Minister Winston Churchill, who led Britain through the darkest days of World War II, was thought to have "limited intelligence" when he was a boy. Ranked last in his class at twelve, he flunked the entrance exam for the Royal Military College at Sandhurst—twice.

Later, he saved the free world from tyranny and annihilation. Makes you wonder what the people at the head of the class might have done.

●●●

What do you learn at law school? As writer Doris Lessing explained, "In university they don't tell you that the greater part of the law is learning to tolerate fools."

●●●

If you learn the lessons of life, this is the educational path you may follow, as described by politician Harold Macmillan:

"The young fool has first to grow up to be an old fool to realize what a damn fool he was when he was a young fool."

●●●

Were you good at taking tests in school? Consider this view from educator Stanley Garn: "If the Aborigine drafted an IQ test, all of Western civilization would presumably flunk it."

Get Me Rewrite!
Eighteen Dumb Newspaper Headlines

1. **Survey Finds Dirtier Subways After Cleaning Jobs Were Cut**
   —from the *New York Times*

2. **Study Finds Sex, Pregnancy Link**
   —from the *Cornell Daily Sun*

3. **Low Wages Said Key to Poverty**
   —from *Newsday*

4. **Malls Try to Attract Shoppers**
   —from the *Baltimore Sun*

5. **Official: Only Rain Will Cure Drought**
   —from the *Westport Herald News*

6. **Teenage Girls Often Have Babies Fathered by Men**
   —from the *Oregonian*

7. **Man Shoots Neighbor with Machete**
   —from the *Miami Herald*

8. **Tomatoes Come in Big, Little, Medium Sizes**
   —from the *Daily Progress*

9. **Man Run Over by Freight Train Dies**
   —from the *Los Angeles Times*

10. Free Advice: Bundle Up When Out in the Cold

  —from the *Lexington Herald-Leader*

11. Economist Uses Theory to Explain Economy

  —from the *Collinsville Herald-Journal*

12. Bible Church's Focus Is the Bible

  —from the *Saint Augustine Record*

13. Lack of Brains Hinders Research

  —from the *Columbus Dispatch*

14. How We Feel About Ourselves Is the Core of Self-Esteem, Says Author Louise Hart

  —from the *Sunday Camera* of Boulder, Colorado

15. Fish Lurk in Streams

  —from the *Rochester Democrat and Chronicle*

16. Infertility Unlikely to Be Passed On

  —from the *Montgomery Advertiser*

17. Alcohol Ads Promote Drinking

  —from the *Hartford Courant*

18. Scientists See Quakes in LA Future

  —from the *Oregonian*

And here's the syllabus for the graduate course from historian Edward Gibbon:

"Conversation enriches the understanding, but solitude is the school of the genius."

•••

In 1990 the president of American University resigned after he was caught making obscene phone calls from his office. Maybe no one told him the university had a policy against on-campus sexual harassment.

•••

George W. Bush outlined his plan to be the education president: "We're going to have the best-educated American people in the world."

For once, you can't argue with the president—at least until our education system is bought by a Japanese company.

•••

"An educated man knows the right thing to do at the time it has to be done," scientist Charles Kettering said. "You can be sincere and still be stupid."

•••

If you think our busing regulations are tough, in Southampton, England, a preschooler was forced to go to a school thirty minutes away because the city council ruled he didn't live close enough to a school that was located just down the block.

How could the boy be so close and yet so far away? Because he lived on the thirteenth floor of an apartment building. If you added in the vertical distance, he was out of the district.

"I think it's pathetic," his mother said. "I think it's stupid, and I think it's ludicrous." Yes, good points, but remember that's the city council we're talking about.

•••

The scholar William Spooner (whose mixed-up sentences gave us spoonerisms) once asked a student, "Was it you or your brother who was killed in the war?"

•••

To foil the enemy during the dark days of World War II, the Civil Defense authority posted these orders: "Illumination must be extinguished when premises are vacated."

It took President Franklin Roosevelt to convince the officials that high school English teachers were not running the country. He had the signs changed to: "Put the lights out when you leave."

•••

How does education prepare us for life? As writer M. H. Alderson pointed out, "If at first you don't succeed, you're running about average."

CHAPTER NINE

Felonious Hats, Killer Makeup, and Other Fashion Trends

SOME people would argue that all fashion is idiotic. Oh, that's right—I am those people.

From shoes that can't be walked in to life-threatening hair, fashion is the perfect obsession for people who are one button short of closure.

•••

In 1797 the English haberdasher John Hetherington invented the top hat. First time he wore his creation on the streets of London, he caused a riot.

He was fined by the police for wearing a "tall structure

calculated to frighten timid people." Which is probably why the top hat became so popular.

You'll notice that Hetherington not only created a new fashion, he's also responsible for calling out the fashion police.

●●●

Their clothes shocked their parents. Church authorities condemned the fashion as obscene, particularly their tight stockings that revealed in public the intimate contours of their legs and buttocks.

Of course, we're talking about teenagers of the fourteenth century in Venice—and the shocking stockings were worn by boys, not girls.

●●●

During the first season, before the TV show *Happy Days* became a monster hit, ABC censors wouldn't allow Fonzie to wear a leather jacket. They didn't want him to project a JD image—even though the Fonz was supposed to be a juvenile delinquent (at least by the standards of 1950s TV).

●●●

Georges Clemenceau, premier of France in the early 1900s, insisted he was prepared to handle any crisis that arose at any hour of the day or night.

To maintain a state of total readiness, Clemenceau went to bed in pants, shirt, coat, shoes, and gloves.

Three Whites, One Green:
The One-color People

1. Poet Emily Dickinson wore only white clothes, but few knew it since she seldom left her home. Her fashion was a charming idiosyncrasy in someone so gifted.

2. Then there was Princess Alexandra of Bavaria, another eccentric with an all-white wardrobe. But the princess's charm became questionable when she announced to the court that she had swallowed a grand piano made of glass.

3. Another notorious all-white dresser was Robert Cook, of the seventeenth-century Irish gentry, who had everything from hats to underwear made of white linen. On his farm he only kept white cows and white horses.

4. The Englishman Henry Cope was known as the Green Man in the nineteenth century. He dressed entirely in green, had the furniture and the rooms of his estate painted green, and ate nothing but green food.

Surrealist painter Salvador Dalí had a shoe fetish that began as a child, when he would take his teacher's slipper and wear it as a hat.

•••

Hetty Green, known as the Witch of Wall Street, came from a wealthy family but was raised in secondhand clothes because they were cheaper.

Hetty increased the Green fortune with astute investments in the 1800s but was even tighter with a dime than the rest of her family.

She kept a considerable part of her fortune stuffed into a petticoat sewn with many hidden pockets, which she washed herself every night and wore again every day.

Even though she made millions in a time when a million dollars meant something, she wore fisherman's boots because they were cheap and long-lasting.

•••

Ever hear of a shoe diary? Francis Henry Egerton, the eighth Earl of Bridgewater, kept one in the nineteenth century. He wore a different pair of shoes every day, then had the used shoes arranged in chronological order.

His servants were under strict orders never to clean the shoes, so the earl could look back and reflect upon the weather of any particular day by the condition of the shoes he had worn that day.

Lord Salisbury, prime minister of England in the 1800s, dressed so shabbily that he was once booted out of a casino in Monte Carlo because they thought he was a beggar.

His Sunday dress to church was a bit unusual too: Salisbury wore a woolen glove on top of his head instead of a hat.

•••

Good fashion question from TV reporter Linda Ellerbee: "If men rule the world, why don't they stop wearing neckties?"

•••

"If you tie your necktie around your knee, instead of around your neck, you are imaginative, but you are imaginative in an imbecile way," said critic John Simon, talking about stupid writers. In fashion, the necktie-around-the-knee look either has been, or will be, somebody's idea of style.

•••

In the Middle Ages, a strange shoe fad swept Europe: pointed shoes for men called *poulaines*. As the fashion spread, the pointed toes became longer and longer (up to two feet long among nobles) until men could not walk in them.

This was the shoes' selling point, for it demonstrated that the wearer was so rich he didn't have to work or walk.

Veronica Lake was such a popular movie star during World War II that women across America copied her unusual hair style: straight hair, worn long and falling seductively over one eye.

But many of these stylish women went to work in factories to support the war effort. A series of horrible accidents occurred when Veronica Lake'd women met indifferent machines. Doing her part for the war effort and to protect working women everywhere, Veronica cut her hair.

•••

Makeup can kill. In ancient Greece, women at the height of fashion applied a white powder to their faces to make themselves more attractive. But the powder contained a heavy dose of lead, which poisoned and killed many of the temporarily attractive women who used it.

•••

In the Dark Ages, arsenic was a popular ingredient in makeup. Because sudden, mysterious death from innumerable causes was common at that unenlightened time, the women didn't suspect that their own cosmetics were killing them.

•••

Although women and men have used makeup since ancient times to make themselves seem more desirable, some societies have tried to ban it. In England in the 1700s, a law was passed outlawing makeup; women who wore it could be arrested and tried as witches.

In the late 1800s a fashion for the natural look spread throughout Europe. Women abandoned all their cosmetics.

A French fashion magazine celebrated the new freedom from makeup, declaring: "It hardly seems likely that a time will ever come again in which rouge and lip paint will be employed."

Half of history is the occurrence of that which at one time "hardly seems likely."

•••

Among the ancient Egyptians, queens and princesses wore such large, elaborate wigs that wig slaves were required to help them walk through the palace.

•••

While wigs were popular with wealthy Europeans for hundreds of years, the clergy often tried to get people out from under their fake hair. In 692 the Church excommunicated people who wore wigs.

Didn't work. Even bald clergy favored wigs. By the 1600s, the French king employed forty wig makers in his court.

•••

Buttons of gold and silver became a trend among French royalty in the sixteenth century. King Francis I paraded through court in a velvet outfit adorned with 13,000 gold buttons.

Francis had to be a strong king because that's roughly a hundred pounds of buttons.

During Queen Elizabeth's reign in England, the government passed a law that people must wear hats. Another attempt by the fashion police to legislate style? Not this time. That law was enacted to stimulate business for felt manufacturers, who had fallen on hard times.

●●●

Although men have worn hats for centuries, writer and professional opinionator P. J. O'Rourke thinks they have all made a moronic mistake.

"A hat should be taken off when you greet a lady and left off for the rest of your life," he expounded. "Nothing looks more stupid than a hat."

●●●

Dumb teenage fads—a thing of the past? Yes, also the present and the future. Back in the 1940s, boys in small American towns wore their car club letter sewn about a foot high across the butt of their jeans.

●●●

Actor Cesar Romero believed that to live well you must dress well. And never in the same outfit. His closets held thirty tuxedos, two hundred sports jackets, and five hundred suits.

What in the world does anyone need five hundred suits for? Four hundred, 450 I can see. But five hundred? Absurd!

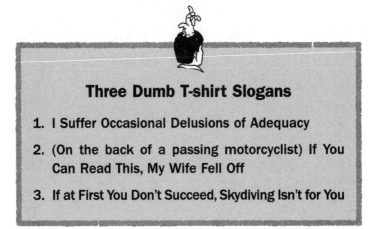

Three Dumb T-shirt Slogans

1. I Suffer Occasional Delusions of Adequacy

2. (On the back of a passing motorcyclist) If You Can Read This, My Wife Fell Off

3. If at First You Don't Succeed, Skydiving Isn't for You

A Singapore hairdresser started a hot, but brief, fad when he figured out a way to cut hair using a blowtorch.

●●●

In 1988 a Japanese company marketed six-day underwear, which you rotated forty degrees a day for three days, then turned inside out for three more days.

Exactly why was this worth the trouble?

●●●

Louis XIV wasn't crazy about baths. The French king took exactly zero baths in his life. Now you know why the French became experts in making perfumes.

The world's first dry cleaners opened in Paris in 1855. First, the cleaner would completely unstitch your clothes. Then he soaked everything in turpentine and oil. Then sewed all your clothes back together.

Or you could just have the silly thing washed.

• • •

In 1999, a tailor in Seoul, South Korea, came up with the idea of manufacturing scented suits for businessmen.

When you pressed a spot on the suit, hidden capsules released the scent of a pine forest. Or peppermint or lavender, if you preferred. To some people, this actually sounded like a good idea.

• • •

In the 1800s, a gentleman was expected to know all thirty-two different ways to knot his tie. No wonder people lived at a slower pace. They dedicated all their free time to their ties.

• • •

A man in France once left money in his will to buy clothes for snowmen.

• • •

In 2002 a Japanese company manufactured underwear that was supposed to reduce fat in your thighs through a mix of seaweed and caffeine rubbed into the fabric.

Must have been tough for Japanese consumers to decide whether they should wear their undershorts or eat them.

When short-short hot pants became a hot fad in the 1960s, Vegas singer Sammy Davis Jr. and his wife showed themselves in public wearing matching hot-pant tuxedos.

●●●

In the fifteenth century, conspicuous excess was considered a privilege of the royal class, and it showed up in their clothes. The Duke of Orléans was a French trendsetter who once had a favorite song embroidered on the sleeve of his cloak, using seven hundred pearls to write the lyrics.

●●●

Whatever French King Louis XI was wearing any time he heard bad news, he never wore those clothes again.

●●●

In Spain during the Middle Ages, ruffs were popular on clothes. But it was against Spanish law for ruffs to be made of anything but white linen, and the pleats had to be no wider than three inches.

●●●

J. Edgar Hoover once fired an FBI agent because he didn't like the man's tie.

CHAPTER TEN

The Business of Stupidity
and Vice Versa

THINK your boss is mean? All bosses will have to work over-time to catch up to these two trendsetters:

1. Millionaire John D. Rockefeller gave his grounds-keepers a Christmas bonus: five dollars each! Then he docked them five dollars each for not working on Christmas Day.

2. John Patterson, founder of National Cash Register, devised odd ways of firing employees who incurred his disfavor. One executive learned he was fired when he arrived at the office and found his desk and chair set ablaze in front of the building.

Welcome to the business world.

Half a million Americans use counterfeit credentials or counterfeit diplomas.

Doesn't it make you wonder how many people with counterfeit diplomas have landed jobs by fooling people with counterfeit credentials?

•••

The phone company promised to send a repairman out the next day to fix a customer's dead phone line, but couldn't be specific about the time. But the company offered to call the customer when the repairman was on the way.

The customer explained that wouldn't do much good since the phone line was dead.

•••

When McDonald's invaded Russia, the American bosses insisted that the Russian counter help give customers the standard Mickey D smile, which kind of looks like an old hamburger curling up at the edges, doesn't it?

Anyway, Russian customers were outraged and insulted because in Russia smiling at strangers means you're making fun of them.

How did Mickey D Russia solve the problem? They hired official Smile Explainers to shout into bullhorns at customers in line (everyone's always in line in Russia): "When you reach the counter, you will be smiled it. This does not mean we are making fun of you."

And that's how Russia became the friendly country it is today.

The basic problem with the free enterprise system is that it often rewards the wrong people with the money. As in, people who are not me.

As economist Walter Bagehot pointed out, "At particular times a great deal of stupid people have a great deal of stupid money."

●●●

Some people do everything wrong because it's the only way they can come up winners.

Take Timothy Dexter, an uneducated eighteenth-century Massachusetts farmer who became a merchant when he married into money.

Dexter should have lost everything when he invested all his money in gloves, Bibles, and warming pans—then shipped them all to the West Indies.

He had chosen the absolutely wrong market, since the West Indies was not a Christian country and it was hot there—a place where no one had ever worn mittens or needed warming pans.

But just as Dexter's ship arrived, a religious fervor swept the country, and all his Bibles were purchased at high prices. The gloves were sold to Russian merchants, whose ships happened to be in port at the same time as Dexter's.

But no one wanted the warming pans, so they were dumped in a warehouse. Then a local farmer discovered that if he threw out the lid, the pan made an ideal ladle for processing molasses. As the island's molasses production grew, Dexter had the only molasses ladles available. So he made another killing he didn't deserve.

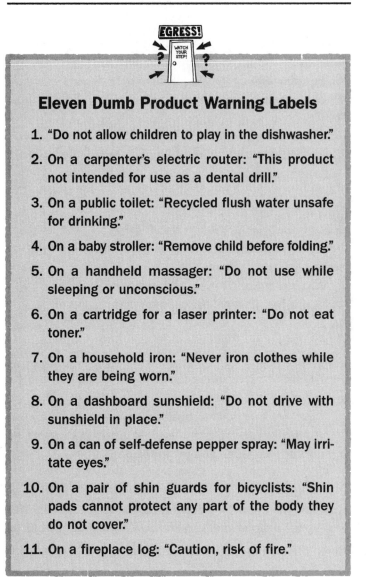

Eleven Dumb Product Warning Labels

1. "Do not allow children to play in the dishwasher."

2. On a carpenter's electric router: "This product not intended for use as a dental drill."

3. On a public toilet: "Recycled flush water unsafe for drinking."

4. On a baby stroller: "Remove child before folding."

5. On a handheld massager: "Do not use while sleeping or unconscious."

6. On a cartridge for a laser printer: "Do not eat toner."

7. On a household iron: "Never iron clothes while they are being worn."

8. On a dashboard sunshield: "Do not drive with sunshield in place."

9. On a can of self-defense pepper spray: "May irritate eyes."

10. On a pair of shin guards for bicyclists: "Shin pads cannot protect any part of the body they do not cover."

11. On a fireplace log: "Caution, risk of fire."

But wait, that's not all. Our fabulously inept businessman Timothy Dexter was fooled into loading a ship with coal from Virginia and sending it to England, to the town of Newcastle.

Yes, coals to Newcastle, the coal-mining capital of Great Britain.

But Dexter's phenomenal luck held: As his ship arrived, the coal miners went out on strike, and Dexter sold his entire load at a high profit.

•••

Will the real dummy please stand up? AT&T fired its president, John Walter, after nine months on the job, saying he lacked intellectual leadership.

Walter received a $26 million severance package. If that's not intellectual leadership, then the world can get along without it.

•••

Does it take brains to succeed in business? Or do they just get in the way?

"The brain is a wonderful organ," poet Robert Frost pointed out. "It starts the moment you get up in the morning and does not stop until you get to the office."

•••

A Boston man was considered a fool in 1903 when he was fired from a railroad after taking a train for a joyride. When he went to work as a stable hand, he was fired for not taking care of the horses. Then he tried his hand as a deliveryman, but lost that job for losing packages.

But that fool, Alfred Fuller, became a millionaire by going to work for himself, selling household products door-to-door as the Fuller Brush Man.

•••

Ford Motor Company invested heavily in launching its new car, the Edsel, back in 1958. The only thing Ford didn't do was find out first that the Edsel was exactly the kind of car no one wanted.

The company lost a quarter billion before they gave it up. For the few people who did buy Edsels, there was a silver lining to the fiasco: There was only a single report of anyone stealing an Edsel.

Ford had managed to design a car that even thieves didn't want.

•••

When showman P. T. Barnum opened his museum of oddities, he did such a good job that people didn't want to leave. They hung around gawking at his exhibits so long that he couldn't get enough new customers in the door.

Barnum finally ran into the main room and banged open the exit door, shouting, "This way to the egress. Folks, see the greatest egress in the world."

When people rushed out, thinking they were going to see a new marvel, Barnum slammed the door behind them. He left them all in the alley, without a dictionary to look up the word *egress*, as he went around front to sell more tickets.

●●●

Victoria Woodhull was the first woman to run for president of the United States, which she did in 1870, long before women were allowed to vote.

Before Woodhull turned to politics, she was a spiritualist, conducting séances for wealthy clients and preaching free love. When that failed to produce enough income, she opened up a stock brokerage and served the same wealthy clientele, this time becoming rich—although her stock advice was no more successful than her spiritual advice.

●●●

In Tacoma, Washington, a woman went into a drugstore to get her prescription refilled for painkillers for her brain tumor.

The pharmacist thought it was a fake prescription, so he called the cops and had her arrested.

The woman tried to explain that she got the same refill at the same store every month. But no one would listen. She asked them to call her doctor. But they hauled her off to jail instead. Can you see the lawsuit coming?

Phone company AT&T has a division that provides cable TV for parts of California. When a customer called the cable office to inquire about programming changes, a clerk told him he'd have to get the information by going down to the company's office.

When the man explained that he simply wanted their phone number, the clerk said, "You have to go there, they don't accept phone calls."

"Excuse me. AT&T doesn't accept phone calls?"

•••

In the 1960s, marketers tried to sell Americans on the idea that what they really needed to make their lives easier was a toothbrush with an aerosol tube embedded in the handle to speed up the toothpaste-loading procedure.

When time management and productivity consciousness come to your toothbrush, your life is already under far too much control.

•••

If you think protest marches were invented by a consortium of hippies and the promoters of the Vietnam War, consider that in 1946 Philadelphia children took to the streets in passionate protest marches.

Their cause? Stores had doubled the price of bubble gum, from one penny to two.

Five Things That Didn't Click Even Though They Aren't That Much Dumber Than Things That Did

1. paper dresses

2. GTO muscle shoes

3. Dear Ear ear makeup

4. Knee Glo knee makeup

5. refrigerator racing

If you want to be successful in business, remember never to let the facts get in your way. Truth is only one option.

In 1913 a factory worker from Illinois named Marshall Gardner published a book that advanced the theory that the earth was hollow. A small interior sun provided light and energy, Gardner claimed, and you could enter this inner world through huge holes at the north and south poles.

Although he had no facts to support his views (which weren't even original), Gardner's book was a big hit. He then became popular on the lecture tour and never went back to factory work again.

Like many American newspaper publishers, William Randolph Hearst never let the facts get in the way of selling more papers.

In 1913 Hearst ran front-page photos of Mexican children standing in a river with their hands raised. The story explained that the kids were surrendering to Mexican federales, who then shot them dead.

The photo and shocking report sold papers, even though the photographer took the shot in Honduras (not Mexico) and the children weren't killed. The reason they had their hands raised was because he asked them to wave for the camera.

•••

William Randolph Hearst also ran phony photos of Russian peasants starving on the streets. The photos turned out to be of famine victims taken years before and not even in Russia.

•••

Hearst wasn't the only newspaperman who resorted to fake news to sell papers. In 1835 editor Richard Locke pumped up sales of the *New York Sun* with a phony series about a scientist whose advanced telescope had spotted life on the moon, creatures that were half man, half bat.

Scientists didn't believe the *Sun's* stories because their telescopes weren't powerful enough even to scan the surface of the moon, much less find creatures on it. But the public bought the hoax, making the *Sun* the most popular paper in the city.

Locke's greatest trick: getting other newspapers to buy into the phony story and print their own reports of moon people who never existed.

•••

"Quite a few people are already working four-day weeks," newspaper columnist Earl Wilson pointed out. "Trouble is, it takes them five or six days to do it."

•••

The English minister Reverend John "Mad Jack" Alington was kicked off his pulpit for preaching free love in the nineteenth century. So he simply started his own church, drawing a congregation by providing free brandy and beer.

During services, Mad Jack would dress in leopard skins and have servants pull him up and down the aisles while he preached astride a wooden hobbyhorse.

•••

When Domino's Pizza ran a promotion in 1988 promising customers they would deliver pizza within thirty minutes, eighteen hustling delivery drivers died in car crashes.

•••

During the winter of 1979, the Allied Roofing Company of Grand Rapids, Michigan, developed a lucrative sideline clearing store roofs of snow to prevent the heavy snowfall from collapsing the roofs.

But one Grand Rapids business did have its roof collapse from snow buildup. That's right, the Allied Roofing Company roof.

•••

Book publishers are in the business of knowing which manuscripts are good enough to publish, right? Well, every now and then. But they also reject plenty of books that go on to become best-sellers for someone else.

Hans Christian Andersen's *Fairy Tales*, now considered a classic, was rejected by every publisher he could find. So the author had to publish the collection at his own expense.

Same story for Daniel Defoe's *Robinson Crusoe*.

Pearl Buck's *The Good Earth* was turned down by twelve publishers.

J. P. Donleavy's *The Ginger Man* was sent back thirty-six times before it was finally published to great success.

•••

French tailor Barthelemy Thimmonier invented one of the first sewing machines in 1830. He was run out of town, and all his machines were destroyed by a mob of angry tailors, who thought his sewing machines would put them all out of work.

About the same time, an American inventor named Walter Hunt developed a sewing machine, but he never pursued the idea because he was afraid it would put tailors out of work.

Hunt also invented the safety pin and sold the rights to it for four hundred dollars.

•••

In the eighteenth century the Luddites of England destroyed new weaving machines when manufacturers installed them. The Luddites thought they could preserve their old ways of life if they could only get rid of the replacement machines. They were wrong, and Luddite-minded people have been wrong ever since.

•••

When toilet paper was invented in 1857, no one in America bought it. People were happy using newspaper and store catalogs instead.

•••

Bankers are highly trained professionals—no, really. An Australian bank gave a woman a thirty-year loan to buy her first home. The woman was ninety-two years old at the time, so she won't have to pay off the loan until she's 122. Now where can we get hold of that banker?

•••

Why is the ducktail big in Bulgaria? A bankrupt Bulgarian company paid off employees' salaries with hundreds of cheap plastic combs because that's all they had left after the money ran out.

"I can throw a comb away every time I comb my hair, and I've still got enough for the rest of my life," one worker said.

•••

As Hitler rose to power in Germany, the United States grew concerned that if American companies sold helium for German zeppelins, the Nazis might use the fuel for military advantage.

So the American supplier—the only source of helium in the world—priced the gas too high for the German company that ran the *Hindenburg*.

Making one of history's dumbest business decisions, the *Hindenburg*'s operators filled the huge blimp with hydrogen instead.

Hydrogen is the perfect gas to use if you want to start a really big fire. Which is exactly what happened after the *Hindenburg* crossed the Atlantic and was trying to dock in New Jersey.

A stray spark ignited the hydrogen, and the blimp burst into flame, burning to its shell in less than a minute, costing thirty-five lives and putting an end to the zeppelin business.

•••

To promote a B-movie called *His Kind of Woman*, producer Howard Hughes built a special billboard on Sunset Boulevard. To show fans just how hot the movie would be, hidden jets shot out gas flames from the bodies of the stars.

The billboard worked once, then Hughes shut it down. The movie wasn't so hot either.

The first pilots' licenses were issued in France in 1909 to sixteen pilots. Not one of them was required to take a test or prove that he could actually fly a plane, safely or otherwise. You may think you've flown with some of those pilots.

•••

In 2003, two airline pilots, who may have been descendants of those first French airmen, were fired for flying naked—even though they explained they were just playing a joke on the stews.

•••

To keep teenage boys from hanging around out front, in 1990 7-Elevens began to pipe elevator music into their parking lots.

That got rid of the skateboarders and slouch champions. But all of a sudden convenience-store parking lots were filled with junior executives and support staff wandering around aimlessly, asking someone to push the button for twenty-seven. Or not.

•••

History's first advertisement appeared on walls in Egypt about three thousand years ago: a notice offering a reward for the return of a runaway slave. Advertising has attempted to enslave people psychologically ever since.

•••

According to the United Nations, the ten richest men in the world have more money than five countries apiece. The top 447 millionaires are richer than half of everyone else.

Three Reasons Advertising Is More Effective If You're Selling to Idiots

1. Showman P. T. Barnum didn't invent the side-show of freaks, but he did invent the way to make a fortune from it—through advertising, which he defined as "selling the public on the idea of throwing away the things they need and buying the things they don't need. So far it's made me a rich man."

2. Writer Stephen Leacock nailed advertising as "the science of arresting the human intelligence long enough to get money from it."

3. Writer George Orwell took the glamor right out of the ad biz when he said, "Advertising is the rattling of a stick inside a swill bucket."

In 1988, when he was still kicking up a rock 'n' roll storm, an Austrian company tried to acquire future rights to Mick Jagger's body.

The company planned to cremate Jagger and pack the ashes into hourglasses to sell to Rolling Stones fans.

In 2002 an Australian bank called the Bank of New Zealand switched from paying lousy interest on savings accounts to giving account owners lottery tickets instead.

You're probably not going to make money either way. But with lottery tickets at least you can enjoy a remote chance of getting rich.

Just asking, but shouldn't the Bank of New Zealand be a New Zealand bank?

•••

A Thai company called Anything You Can Think Of provided unusual services for its clients, including engaging in arguments, slapping your enemies, or providing professional mourners to cry at your funeral.

If you wanted Anything agents to argue with your enemies while slapping amateur mourners, that was extra.

•••

Opera singer Giovanni Martinelli once appeared in a cigarette advertisement, even though he was a nonsmoker. The ad promised smokers that their brand did not irritate the throat.

"How could it irritate my throat?" Martinelli explained. "I have never smoked."

CHAPTER ELEVEN

Dumb Crooks:
Quick, Let's Hop on the Motorized
Bar Stool and Make Our Getaway

DUMB crooks are good for the economy. If it weren't for the stupid criminals, we'd need twice as many cops to catch the smart ones.

So let's all give a round of applause to those crooks putting out that extra effort to get into prison.

●●●

A robbery suspect in an LA lineup got incensed when cops asked the other men in the lineup to say, "Give me all your money or I'll shoot."

"That's not what I said!" the suspect corrected them.

Okay, the rest of you guys in line can go home now.

A Swedish woman got out of a tax fraud charge when she convinced the court that rats in her attic ate all her financial records. But the rat got five to ten.

●●●

England in the nineteenth century was a rough place to be a criminal, or even suspected as a criminal. Among the reasons judges condemned people to be hung: cutting down a tree, damaging a pond, associating with gypsies, writing on a bridge, and walking in public with a dirty face.

●●●

When a pharmacist in Santa Cruz, California, opened up shop one morning, he saw a pair of legs dangling from the ceiling inside the store. He found a burglar stuck in the ceiling vent.

The man told police he was walking his dog on the roof of the pharmacy and had accidentally fallen through. Police arrested him anyway—just another case of cops harassing a guilty man.

●●●

In 2003, a Pennsylvania couple dressed their seven-year-old son in a Cub Scout uniform and went door to door through their town raising money for his scout troop.

Doesn't sound like a crime? The boy wasn't a Cub Scout, and there was no such troop.

They conned 150 neighbors out of $667 before they got caught. How? They knocked on the door of an Eagle Scout, who saw right away that the parents had knotted the boy's tie. Cub Scouts use scout slides on their ties, not knots. Hey, it's all right there in the manual.

•••

If you owe the bill collectors and they don't believe you when you said the check was in the mail (and they won't buy the one about your dog eating the bill), not to worry. The post office is here to help with a great excuse.

In 1989, mail inspectors in Boulder, Colorado, found that one of their carriers had buried 6,500 pounds of mail in his backyard instead of delivering it. Oddly enough, he wasn't awarded a medal.

•••

In Port Royal, Virginia, in 2003, a bank robber set a record for botching the job, sprint division. He robbed a bank, then left a trail of dropped $100 bills all the way out to his car.

When he got to the car, he couldn't make his getaway because he had locked the keys inside. He tried to break a window but wasn't strong enough to smash the glass.

When he saw people from the bank coming after him, the bank robber fled on foot. When they caught up with him, he turned his gun on them . . . and shot himself in the leg. Finally, the cops came to give him a break and take him to jail.

In 2001, a man in North Carolina called police to complain that a thief had stolen his marijuana plants. When the police showed up, the victim led them into his garden, where the thief had ripped out the illegal pot plants.

Wait! It gets dumber, because the thief hadn't ripped out all the plants. Growing in the garden were another twenty-two pot plants worth millions. The police led the man off to jail when they were able to stop giggling.

•••

Two Michigan store owners started a fire to burn up their inventory, which wasn't selling, and collect on the insurance. But the fire got out of control and burned the store next door.

The men who set the fire then sued the insurance company, arguing that the second fire was an accident and should be covered by their policy. They lost the suit.

•••

In 2003, an inventive if dim-witted crook robbed a Wiener-schnitzel fast food restaurant in Long Beach, California. To disguise himself, he smeared chocolate pudding all over his face.

Maybe if he'd used mustard, the robber would have blended in with the scene of the crime and gotten away with it.

•••

A man in New Zealand was arrested for setting his underwear on fire and riding through town on a motorized bar stool. The charge? Driving without a license.

In Illinois a man kidnapped a driver at gunpoint and forced him to drive to two automated teller machines. But the gunman didn't steal any of the driver's money. Instead, the almost-not-a-crook withdrew money from his own bank accounts.

When caught, the man couldn't be charged with robbery since he hadn't taken anyone else's money. Unfortunately, he was charged with kidnapping.

•••

A robber wasn't satisfied with the take from a holdup at a Topeka convenience store. So he gagged the clerk and worked the front register himself for three hours.

Then just as he made enough money for one night's work, the cops showed up at the store and busted him.

This is one of those rare crimes where the thief actually made money for the victim.

•••

Some dumb crimes are notable for the stupidity not of the crooks but of their victims.

In 1906, a poor German shoemaker named William Voight pulled off one of the most daring stunts in history. First, he spent all the money he had left on a used army captain's uniform. Then he took a train to a small town and ordered the soldiers on duty there to arrest the town officials for fraud. Finally, he collected all the money from the town treasury for evidence.

Such was Voight's air of authority that everyone obeyed his orders. Although he only walked off with a few hundred dollars, his daring crime made him famous. After serving a short jail sentence, he made a small fortune on the vaudeville stage reenacting his audacious fraud.

•••

Police in Oakland, California, surrounded a house where a gunman had barricaded himself inside. When they couldn't talk him out, the cops shot tear gas canisters through the windows.

But nothing happened until the police found that the gunman was standing outside right next to them, calling toward the house, "Please come out and give yourself up."

•••

A snatch-and-grab thief in Chicago decided to see how much he could scoop up from the display window of a jewelry store. But first he needed to break the window.

No problem. He pried a manhole cover out of the street and smashed it through the window. He grabbed jewelry and took off running. And he might have gotten away with his crime if he hadn't fallen down the open manhole.

•••

A German blackmailer came up with an original scheme to extort money from the Nestlē Company. He ordered company executives to place diamonds in tiny bags, then tie them around the necks of homing pigeons.

He was captured when the police simply followed the pigeons to their destination.

You don't have to be a politician to spin history. Here's Abu Abbas explaining away the murder of an American hostage in a wheelchair when Palestinian terrorists hijacked a cruise ship in 1985: "The media didn't tell the world that Abu Abbas saved the lives of six hundred passengers, only that a disabled man was killed."

He didn't specify what the appropriate ratio of people you don't kill to people you do kill should be to merit the world's thanks.

●●●

Wonder why jails are overcrowded? Because people like this insist on filling them.

In 2002, a Michigan shoplifter dropped her handbag as she was chased from a store. She later called the police to see if anyone had turned in her purse.

"You're in luck," an officer told her. When she showed up at the station to get her purse, the cops busted her.

●●●

Introduction to Robbery 101: Two crooks in Italy stole a car at gunpoint from a woman who was waiting in line at a gas station.

The cops caught them a couple miles down the road. Why? The crooks forgot the first rule of getaways: Don't steal the car *before* the driver fills it up with gas.

Perhaps the third time's the charm. A Colorado bandit robbed the same convenience store twice in the same day, then told the clerk he'd be back after she made more money.

The robber actually did return and was arrested by the cops, who were still questioning the clerk about the first two robberies.

●●●

In 1978, a Baltimore robber found a unique way to get himself arrested. When the woman he was robbing didn't have much cash on her, he suggested she write him a check.

She did, and the police simply traced the cashed check back to the robber.

●●●

In Massachusetts police had an easy time arresting a bank robber who got so nervous during the holdup that he fainted.

●●●

In 1983, two Arizona men were having car trouble on the side of the highway. Yes, they had been drinking. No, no one driving by stopped to help them.

So they figured out a great way to get people to stop: They took out their guns and shot at passing cars. And someone did stop—the cops.

●●●

The irony is more than we asked for. The founder of a group that helps people with drinking problems pleaded guilty in

2000 to vehicular homicide after hitting two people while driving drunk. Her group, Moderation Management, claims that moderate drinking can work for some drunks.

•••

In 1988 John Zaccaro Jr. was given a four-month sentence for selling cocaine. He spent three months of that detention living in a luxury condo in Burlington, Vermont. But as his mother pointed out: "He didn't have a maid."

Remember his mom? Geraldine Ferraro, who ran for vice president on the Democratic ticket with Walter Mondale.

•••

In California last year the San Bernardino County sheriff's department sent offers to people wanted on felony warrants for free hiking boots made by "Stockdum Scelestus."

What none of the felons who showed up figured out was that the manufacturer's name was a mix of German and Latin that meant "utterly stupid criminal."

That's what the felons must have felt like when instead of being given free boots, they were busted.

•••

The nineteenth-century British aristocrat John Mytton carried too much money with him for someone who drank so heavily in taverns. He was known as an easy mark for robbers.

But nineteenth-century highwaymen weren't necessarily any smarter than rich drunks. As Mytton left a tavern, he was grabbed by rival gangs at the same time and became the rope in a larcenous tug of war.

Neither side would let go of their quarry, so Mytton, in his drunken strength, knocked them all down and held several of them until the police arrived.

•••

Big Brother is also watching Big Brother. In 2002, cameras used to catch speeders in Holland were destroyed by angry drivers. So the police tried to catch the vandals by installing new sets of cameras to watch the other cameras.

•••

Neighbors in the town of Offenbach, Germany, thought a horrible crime must be happening when they heard the screams from next door. So they called the police.

When the cops got inside the home, they found a seventy-six-year-old woman practicing her yodeling.

"The officers weren't able to judge whether the neighbors were unfamiliar with Bavarian folk music," the police report concluded, "or whether the lady still requires a lot of practice."

•••

Even when they do go to prison, corporate big shots still live better than most people do outside prison.

That's why *Forbes* magazine reviewed the best prisons in America, the minimum-security jails for white-collar criminals, evaluating them on their accommodations, food, and such amenities as recreational and athletic facilities.

CHAPTER TWELVE

Dumb Ways to Die:
Buried Alive but Not for Long

MOST OF us manage to die without the help of harmonicas and lions. We don't tempt fate with our bathing suits. We feel no need to exert our mental powers on speeding trains.

But if there weren't plenty of people who volunteered to run the gamut to dumb deaths, these pages would be blank.

•••

In 1937, the Reverend Harold Davidson went on a hunger strike after the Church of England defrocked him for consorting with prostitutes. He was then arrested for attempted suicide, a crime in England.

As the trial began, he had himself hauled into court locked in a cage with a lion. This was Davidson's idea of a publicity stunt that was supposed to gain him popular sympathy.

Before Davidson could take the stand to prove his innocence, the lion killed him.

●●●

In the eighteenth century, an Italian duke named Antonio Fernando was told by a fortune teller that alcohol would be the death of him. So he stopped drinking.

One night Fernando used an alcohol rub to soothe his aching muscles. The alcohol caught fire and he burned to death.

●●●

In the 1800s, European doctors recommended that patients take to the waters at the seashore, lakes, and springs for their health. Modesty demanded that women wear bathing suits with underlayers made of flannel, topped by skirts, bloomers, and shoes.

While seeking their health in the water, many women drowned under the weight of their heavy bathing outfits.

●●●

The Indian mystic Khadeshwari Baba had his followers bury him alive in 1980 to demonstrate his remarkable control over body and spirit. When he was dug up ten days later, he was demonstrating his powers on some other plane of existence. On this plane, he was dead.

The evidence may have been circumstantial, but what jury could resist so many coincidences? In 1911, three men were convicted of murdering Sir Edmund Berry at Greenberry Hill.

The killers were hanged for their crime. Their names weirdly enough: Green, Berry, and Hill.

•••

Here's a dumb way to be forced to die. Lawyers for a death row inmate in Arkansas appealed to federal court in 2003 that their client should not be executed because he was insane and a Supreme Court decision prohibits execution of the insane.

But the appeals court ruled that the prisoner should be given antipsychotic drugs involuntarily so that he would return to sanity and could then be legally executed.

As the judge wrote, explaining the court's decision: "Eligibility for execution is the only unwanted consequence of the medication."

Can't you see the prescription warning label: "Side effects may include nausea, dizziness, anxiety, impotence, and eligibility for execution."

•••

A psychic healer in Russia, known as E. Frenkel, wanted to demonstrate his ability to stop a train using only the power of his remarkable mind. So in 1998, he stepped in front of a freight train.

Brakes eventually stopped the train, but long after Frenkel had learned the bumpy limitations of his psychic powers.

Musicians often add novelty items to their acts to draw audience attention. Ramon Barrero, a Mexican musician, had a clever gimmick: playing a tiny harmonica so small you could barely see it when he played it.

Unfortunately, in 1994 the harmonica slipped from his fingers as Barrero inhaled and he choked to death on stage.

•••

In 1902, the scorekeeper at a baseball game in Morristown, Ohio, was sharpening his pencil with a knife when a foul ball was lined back into the stands. As unlikely as it sounds, the ball slammed into the scorekeeper's hand, hammered the knife into his chest, and killed him.

•••

An Illinois woman died in 1996 when she was smothered in the trash. But she didn't die in a tragic garbage can accident or down at the dump.

The woman was an obsessive collector of trash, piling it up inside her house. One day the trash piles collapsed on top of her.

•••

Matthew Webb was the first person to swim across the English Channel and live. It took him nearly twenty-two hours to make the arduous crossing in 1875. His achievement was hailed internationally.

Eight years later he got the bright idea of swimming

across the waters above Niagara Falls. He died when he was swept over the falls. Wouldn't have become incrementally more famous if he had succeeded.

●●●

In 1989, not one but two people got so angry at unfulfilling vending machines that they grabbed the offending machines and shook them to get out their purchases. The machines toppled over and killed them—two rare cases of death by vending machine.

●●●

One tastes like chickpeas, the other bubbles. An Israeli man died at ninety-one when his nurse spread dishwashing detergent on his bread instead of the chickpea spread hummus.

The nurse told police he couldn't read the Hebrew writing on the detergent container.

●●●

But did he reach level five? A game-loving Korean man played computer games for eighty-six hours without stopping to eat or sleep. Then he died, having gamed himself to death.

●●●

In 1705, the people of West Hartlepool, England, thought they had captured a French spy, so they hung him. The "spy" was an ape. Not a big dumb guy—a real ape.

Two Tough Ways to Almost Die

1. In 1906, a man named Alfredo Bindi tried to commit suicide by eating his suspenders. He failed.

2. In 2000, an Italian man tried to drown himself in a river, but was swept away into the Milan sewer system instead. He floated in the "stinking, filthy water" for six hours before rescuers pulled him out through a manhole.

George II of England died after falling off his throne. But it wasn't so noble. The throne he fell off of was his toilet.

A Zimbabwe spiritual leader drowned during a tribal rite in 1990. His followers didn't pull him out of the water because they thought his magical powers were protecting him, enabling him to breathe underwater, where he lay for two days.

•••

In 1990 a hunter wounded a deer, but the deer wouldn't quit. So the man clubbed it with his shotgun, which fired by accident, killing the hunter.

In Virginia in 2003, a man was bit by a dog. He went after the mutt with a rifle, determined to beat the dog to death with the butt of the gun.

You can see this one coming, can't you? While the man was thumping the dog, the rifle went off and the man shot himself to death. The dog recovered nicely.

●●●

In 1989, a man in Connecticut called his wife a "fat ox," but shouldn't have. Upset, she stumbled, fell, and landed on top of him. Before she managed to get off, he was crushed to death. She weighed 500 pounds.

●●●

In 1899, an Englishman was taken by a car salesman on the first demo ride in British history. The salesman crashed the car, killing them both. It was the first car collision in history in which someone other than the driver died.

●●●

In the sixteenth century, Sir Richard Grenville, captain of the English ship *Revenge*, took on twenty Spanish galleons and refused to surrender, even when his ship had been riddled by eight hundred cannonballs and all his men were dead or wounded.

Instead, Grenville smashed a wine glass, then ate the glass and bled to death.

Millions of peasants in the Soviet Union were starved to death in the famine years of 1932 to 1934 even though they would have survived if they had been allowed to eat the food they grew.

They died not because there wasn't enough food but because it was politically expedient. Soviet dictator Josef Stalin wanted to demonstrate the success of his collective farms by exporting the grain harvest around the world. Incidentally, he denied his own people the food that would have kept them alive.

●●●

If you were a good athlete in Central America in ancient times, you probably played *tlachtli*, especially if you were a slave athlete.

The game pitted two teams that hit a ball without using hands or feet—tricky business. But you wanted to be skillful at it since the losing team was slaughtered after the game.

That's why team owners used slaves. Can't you see wheels spinning at the NFL?

CHAPTER THIRTEEN

Oofty Goofty, Screaming Meemies, and Other Amazing Acts of Popped Culture

COMPOSER John Cage wrote a song called "As Slow as Possible." Cage's idea: the song would take 629 years to play.

And they say pop culture has no lasting value.

•••

Most kids think their fathers are idiots at one time or another. But most dads don't give their kids proof.

Then there's Hollywood. As movie director Billy Wilder pointed out, "A bad play folds and is forgotten, but in pictures we don't bury our dead. When you think it's out of your system, your daughter sees it on television and says, 'My father is an idiot.'"

Among the stranger acts in the history of show business was the display of pain tolerance by a nineteenth-century San Francisco street performer known as Oofty Goofty. For his act, Oofty charged people to punch, kick, and beat him with a bat.

Boxing champ John L. Sullivan took Oofty Goofty up on the offer to hit him with a pool cue for fifty cents. Sullivan broke Goofty's back, and that was the end of his showbiz career.

•••

Two days after the United States invaded Panama to depose the country's ruler, Mañuel Noriega, a computer company released a war game called Find Noriega.

•••

To ring in the new year, a Florida radio station played "Stairway to Heaven" 181 times in a row on December 31, 1989. Dumb enough. But nothing is so dumb that it can't be trumped.

The DJ who played 181 "Stairways" was trumped by the person who listened to them all and kept count, making sure no one was trying to short fans a "Heaven" or two.

•••

Back in the 1950s, Fess Parker's TV show made everything Davy Crockett a hit. Not only did they sell more coonskin hats than anyone ever wore in wild frontier times. But one sporting goods store owner figured out how to sell his stock of 200,000 pup tents.

He simply wrote the name Davy Crockett on the tents and sold them all in two days.

•••

In the 1950s, college students got into a fad that would be all but impossible today: stuffing themselves into phone booths. The record: thirty-four students crammed into a single booth.

Remember phone booths? Think of them as large, clunky cell phones.

•••

Disco fever? Hip-hop frenzy? Nothing compared to the frenetic dance madness that swept through Europe in the Middle Ages.

Today you'd have to pay a crazy fortune for concert tickets and the privilege of dancing yourself into a mind-altering state with hundreds of strangers.

Back then people would suddenly break into wild, convulsive dancing in the streets. Didn't cost them a thing, other than possible imprisonment as witches and such injuries as cobblestone heel.

Think you've danced till the sun comes up? The medieval dance craze lasted for two hundred years, into the sixteenth century.

To cure dance fever, cities banished the color red from buildings and clothes. It was thought that anything red drove the dancers wild.

Three Tries to
Trash the Rock

1. Talent helps if you're trying to make it in rock 'n' roll, but brains will usually trip you up. As Frank Zappa of the Mothers of Invention pointed out, "The typical rock fan isn't smart enough to know when he's being dumped on."

2. Even though he recorded several rock 'n' roll songs, singer Frank Sinatra didn't care for the music, declaring rock to be "phony and false, sung, written, and played for the most part by cretinous goons."

3. The Guess Who had a hit in 1970 with "Share the Land." But the song was banned across the South because politicians thought it was promoting communism.

   As the band later explained, the song was about heaven. Wouldn't those red-baiting politicians have served the country better by investigating the subversive lyrics in "Louie, Louie"? Oh that's right, they had the FBI handle that investigation.

You've heard of songs that are number one with a bullet? Here's a tune that was number one with a goose.

In 1974, a man in England was listening to a record of Frankie Lane singing "Cry of the Wild Goose" when he heard something crash in his bedroom. He ran into the room and found that a wild goose had flown through the window. Two more geese crashed into the window and bounced off outside. Now that's singing.

•••

Here's a new way to think of the amnesia-inducing empty-headedness of TV: Cellist Gregor Piatigorsky agreed to make his first TV appearance when a friend explained that it would "take over one hundred years for that many people to hear me in concert," the cellist recalled.

"He failed to tell me how many seconds it would take them to forget."

•••

During the Vietnam War, the South Vietnamese government didn't have much luck fighting the Viet Cong. They had more success in the battle against American pop culture, banning the twist because the dance was "not compatible with the anticommunist struggle."

Who would have guessed that at their opening night party, the original cast of *West Side Story* danced to the music from *My Fair Lady*? Oh, those teenage rebels of the fifties.

•••

Don't know how many people listen to music each day, but we do know that every day 80 million people around the world hear Muzak.

•••

When a teenage Bob Dylan and his first rock 'n' roll band played for a dance at his Minnesota high school, the school principal pulled the plug on the singer's microphone.

•••

Composer George Antheil, known as the "bad boy of music," gave avant garde concerts in which a player piano made all the music. Antheil sat at the piano and pretended to play, moving around so aggressively and with so many contortions that he drove himself to the point of total collapse—without actually making any music.

These shows made him the toast of Paris in the 1920s.

•••

John Barrymore was the first American actor to play Hamlet on the London stage. At the premier, he made his entrance drunk out of his mind.

Throughout the play, he had to lean on other actors to keep from falling, and he rushed offstage several times to throw up. To deliver Hamlet's famous "To be, or not to be" speech, Barrymore staggered to a chair and sat down so he wouldn't fall down.

The English critics raved—not *at* Barrymore, *for* him. They thought his drunken maneuvers created a masterful interpretation of Hamlet, especially his daring, seated presentation of the "to be or not to be" speech.

•••

In the eighteenth century, Robert Coates was considered by critics and audiences to be the worst Shakespearean actor anyone had ever seen. When he played Romeo, the London audience responded with a barrage of garbage. The star had to crawl offstage to escape.

But Coates had his revenge. His performance was so ludicrous that six people in the audience laughed themselves sick and had to be hospitalized. That may have been the first and only time *Romeo and Juliet* was interpreted as a comedy.

•••

During the Great Depression, flagpole sitting became an unusual and incredibly foolish fad, sponsored by businesses trying to draw crowds.

Shipwreck Kelly became the most famous flagpole sitter in the United States, setting the world record by swaying atop a pole for forty-nine days and nights. His nickname: The Luckiest Man Alive.

Kelly's record stood for fifty years, primarily because few people were dumb enough to want to break it. Then in 1976, Frank Perkins smashed the record by sitting atop a flagpole at a used car lot for an entire year.

•••

What is it with teenage girls and the need to squeal at high decibels? It's not a rock 'n' roll phenomenon. It goes back at least to the 1940s when girls gathered in cities across the nation to squeal at Frank Sinatra's performances. They were known then as "screaming meemies."

Only after Sinatra's fame was secured was it revealed that his PR guy paid girls to squeal, swoon, and faint at those first shows.

•••

During the reign of King Louis XIII, the place to be seen was the court ballet, where the trendsetters of France strutted about in their most elaborate fashions.

Eventually, so many pretenders spilled onto the stage that there was no room left for the dancers, and performances were canceled. People who went to the ballet never actually saw the ballet. But perhaps it was better that way.

•••

The world's first ballet was performed for the king of France in 1581. It was such an expensive staging (costing over three million gold francs) and lasted so long (five and a half hours) that it was only danced once. Fans have been grateful ever since.

Fiddler on the Roof was banned in Chile for sixteen years. But in 1990, the ban was lifted and Chileans were finally allowed to see the daring musical about Russian Jews, which must have caused a large portion of the Chilean population to go: Huh? We waited sixteen years for that?

•••

Can we open that window for you, Mr. Richards? The Hyatt Hotel in West Hollywood was known as the Riot Hotel in the 1970s because of rockers like Keith Richards, who tossed furniture out the window; Led Zeppelin, who rode their motorcycles up to their rooms; and Jim Morrison, who tempted fate by hanging from balcony railings.

•••

The Best of Click and Clack, heard on the *Car Talk* radio show: "Now for another short break. In other words, it's time for you to scan the dial and see if there's anything less moronic on."

•••

A parting shot from critic Ian Shoales: "When I saw *Annie* I had to hit myself on the head afterward with a small hammer to get that stupid 'Tomorrow' song out of my head."

•••

And yet another parting shot from baseball great Yogi Berra: "It was pretty good. Even the music was nice." Yogi was talking about his first trip to the opera.

CHAPTER FOURTEEN

Anthro-dimology:
The Study of How Stupid
Ancient People Were Before
They Became Us

THE GREAT thing about the past is that we can look back and laugh at them, and they can't laugh back. Time makes us smarter by cutting off the argument in our favor.

•••

Back before we had scientists to explain everything to the rest of us, there were still plenty of know-it-alls who thought they knew how things worked.

Here are some popular beliefs that now look idiotic to our enlightened selves. But I wonder which of our current beliefs will be proven just as dumb when we do the year 3004 edition of this book.

Beekeepers could create new bees by letting veal rot (seventh century).

To have a boy baby, a wife should grind up the male sexual organs of hares and drink them mixed with wine (eleventh century).

Baby bears were blobs at birth and did not become bear-shaped until they were formed into bearlets by their mothers (twelfth century).

Lion cubs remained lifeless after they were born until a male lion breathed on them (thirteenth century).

You could soften diamonds by soaking them in goat blood (seventeenth century). Why you would want a soft diamond in the 1600s was never made entirely clear.

A doctor treating the victim of a sword wound should apply his medicines to the sword instead of the wound (seventeenth century).

Ketchup and mustard led people to uncontrollable lust (nineteenth century). Well, have you been to a Jack-in-the-Box lately?

●●●

In Victorian times, pianos were considered risqué. So in proper English households, skirts were put around pianos to shield their legs.

In England during the Middle Ages, it was considered unmanly to sleep on a mattress or any other soft surface. Real men slept on the floor in their clothes because they thought it made them better fighters.

But real men had trouble explaining why the tough-sleeping English lost several wars to the soft-sleeping French.

●●●

In Italy during the 1500s, men were considered effeminate for eating their food with a fork. So boys, next time your mom scolds you for picking up your food with your hands, just tell her you're a man.

●●●

Even before Emily Post, there were proper manners. But in the Dark Ages in Europe, manners were a little different than they are in today's polite society. Back then if you were a lady or a gentleman, you were expected to adhere to the following rules:

Don't pick your teeth with your knife.

Don't chew on a bone, then put it back in the common dish.

Don't blow your nose on the tablecloth.

Don't spit across the table.

In ancient Europe, people thought that to build a bridge was to tempt fate. So to appease the gods and keep the bridge from collapsing, children were sacrificed, buried alive inside the bridge's foundation.

●●●

We throw rice at the bride, as they did at weddings centuries ago. They also threw wheat to wish the new bride many children.

Oh, and they threw one more thing at weddings. For fertility insurance, well-wishers tossed old shoes at the bride. That's how we get the shoes tied to the rear of cars, a modern relief for shoe-ducking brides everywhere.

●●●

We celebrate Christmas Day as the birth of Christ. But in the third century, the Catholic Church considered it a sin to celebrate Jesus's birth.

Even the attempt to figure out exactly when Jesus was born was labeled sacrilegious.

●●●

During the Dark Ages, kings were the only people who had birthday celebrations. Ordinary people celebrated only the day of their deaths because it marked their escape from this world of woe into a better life in heaven.

In ancient times, the dead were buried in coffins not out of respect but because people feared the deceased would come back and haunt them. That's why coffins were nailed shut.

A large stone was placed on top of the coffin, not as a commemorative tombstone, but to keep the dead from escaping.

•••

Every culture comes up with its own story to explain the creation of the world. All creation stories have, what they call in Hollywood, holes in the plot. But some are more creative than others.

In the South Pacific, people believed that the human race was created from sugar cane, with one bud of the stalk turning into the first man and another bud into the first woman.

This explains why women are so sweet—and why men are so . . . sweet also. No, that doesn't hold. Maybe this story explains why sugar is bad for you.

•••

In the early 1800s, the stylish young upper-class Englishman was known as a dandy, buck, or beau. To be a proper English dandy, you had to throw away all your family money on gambling and elaborate dinner parties.

If you did it right, you went deeply into debt, then fled the country for France when you couldn't pay your bills.

But the one thing you never did, no matter how dire the circumstances, was go to work to pay off your debts. It simply wasn't done in polite society.

If you were traveling back in time to the Middle Ages and could take along only one thing, what would you take?

You probably didn't say a clothespin. But it would come in useful clipped firmly around your nose, because Europe in the Middle Ages was the stinkiest age the human race has yet contrived.

Especially in cities like Paris and London, where people dumped their refuse into the gutters—or on the sidewalks if they had a weak slop pot arm and couldn't reach the gutters.

Most people never bathed; it was considered sinful and unhealthy. They rarely washed their clothes.

If all that wasn't smelly enough, they invented a clever strategy to combat the mice and bugs that shared their straw bedding: They stuffed garlic in with the straw before going to sleep.

●●●

Sometimes those old fairy tales we read to our children are too gruesome for the little ones. If only the kids knew that most of them were actually toned down from the original, centuries-old stories.

In the first version of *Snow White and the Seven Dwarfs*, the wicked queen is punished by being forced into iron shoes. The shoes are then set in a fire until the queen burns up dancing to death.

In the original *Cinderella* tale, the put-upon girl murders her evil stepmother. But her father then marries an even more evil woman.

In another early version, when one of Cinderella's gross stepsisters can't fit her fat foot into the glass slipper, her mother simply hacks off part of her foot—and the shoe fits!

Little Red Riding Hood gets eaten by the wolf (as does her grandmother) in the original tale.

As for Sleeping Beauty, the prince rapes her while she sleeps and she gives birth to twins while still in a coma.

But parents can be relieved because kids don't always pick up on the gruesome nature of these fairy tales. Instead, they may get this interesting message from a lot of fables: Even though adults are in charge of the world, they're dumb and can easily be fooled.

●●●

In the fifteenth century, an English bishop named Reginald Pecock tried to purify the English language by getting rid of words of Latin origin.

His idea ran out of popular steam when he recommended such changes as "inconceivable" to "nottobethoughtable."

●●●

You think our nonsmoking rules are too strict? Or not strict enough?

Consider what happened to the first cigarette smoker in Europe. A sailor in Christopher Columbus's crew, Rodrigo de

Jerez, brought cigarettes back to Europe from his explorations of Cuba.

He also became the new era's first cigarette addict, and the Inquisition threw him into prison for the "devilish habit" of smoking.

•••

Around 1400, the French University of Toulouse wasn't bringing in enough money through student tuition. How did they raise the cash? Not from alumnae. But by opening the Abbaye, a university-sponsored brothel.

•••

Capturing Africans and selling them into slavery was not a barbarism invented by greedy Europeans or American plantation owners. The Islamic world had been enslaving Africans for a thousand years before European capitalists moved in on the slave trade.

•••

We look at ancient Greece for the shining light of freedom and democracy. Yet all the great achievements of that enlightened culture were built on the backs of slave labor. Not only did the Greeks originate the concept of freedom but also the abuse of freedom.

In the Dark Ages, when the poor people of Paris died (often of plagues), they were dumped in unmarked graves in the Cemetery of the Innocents.

In the thirteenth century, that cemetery became a Parisian promenade, where the fashionable shopped and strolled of an evening, past mounds of human bones.

•••

In medieval times the French and the English held low opinions of each other. One popular belief in France was that Englishmen were born with tails.

CHAPTER FIFTEEN

Riding the Bull,
Mourning the Cowwws:
The Wonderful World of
Stupid Eccentricities

CAN YOU be a knucklehead and eccentric at the same time? Sure, if you're willing to put in the extra effort.

Like John Mytton, a nineteenth-century British aristocrat who felt guilty about his inherited wealth. When that happens to the relatively normal rich, they give away some of their money to a worthy cause and usually feel better enough to fly off to the Riviera guilt-free.

Not Mytton. His guilt led him to the odd habit of hunting ducks naked in the snow. One other manifestation of his loose-brained eccentricity—his nickname: Mango, the King of Pickles. No, really.

But Mango was in good company:

Writer Louisa May Alcott's father, Amos, believed in the non-violent and ethical treatment of bugs.

But that didn't make him a good neighbor. When Amos found potato bugs in his garden, he carefully picked them off, but didn't kill them. Instead, he dropped the plant eaters over the fence into his neighbor's garden.

•••

To demonstrate how he earned the nickname the Mouth, Jim Purol smoked 140 cigarettes at the same time in 1983.

For some reason, Purol's attempt to apply economy of scale to the strategy of suicide by cigarette was not recognized by American industry.

•••

Cambridge scholar Charles Ogden disliked being disturbed during his studies, particularly by noise from the street outside his home. To drown the outside noise, he filled his rooms with loud chiming clocks and radios playing at full volume. Then he'd work through the night on his research. He'd have dinner at dawn.

•••

The Christian Apostolic Church was a repressive sect in Zion, Illinois, led by the preacher and General Overseer Wilbur Voliva in the 1880s.

Among his strange personal habits that became the group's commandments: no bacon, no oysters, no humming, no whistling. Everyone had to be indoors by ten p.m., and all of his followers had to agree that the earth was flat.

•••

Actress Sarah Bernhardt always kept a bizarre good luck charm with her when she went on tour: a coffin.

•••

Queen Elizabeth I of England was a charmer in some ways, but for the last ten years of her life she refused to wash her face.

•••

Hermit and artist Edward Leedskalnin spent twenty years creating a coral castle and vast garden of coral sculpture in a remote part of Florida, where few people ever saw his creations.

Although he had no family, Leedskalnin wrote and published a family advice book instructing parents to stop their kids from smiling because it caused wrinkles.

•••

William Hervey, a seventeenth-century doctor to English kings, had an unusual writing habit: He added more letters to the end of words than were needed, so that *cow* became *cowww* and *man* became *mannn*.

Martin van Butchell, a prominent London doctor of the eighteenth century, painted his white horses with purple spots when he rode around town.

•••

Another English eccentric, Sir Tatton Sykes, was obsessed with maintaining body warmth. He would walk through the countryside wearing layers of overcoats, which he simply discarded along the road as the day got warmer.

Village boys made good money following him on his walks, then returning the coats for a shilling apiece, over and over again.

•••

The Archduke Franz Ferdinand of World War I fame despised wrinkles and creases in his clothes. So he had servants sew him into his suits before he appeared in public.

The obsession backfired when Ferdinand was shot by Sarajevo assassins. His people couldn't cut his clothes off quickly enough to stop the bleeding. World War I might have been averted by better buttons.

•••

Matthew Robinson was an eighteenth-century English lord, so he got away with his odd behavior, which was mostly of the watery variety.

A semi-hermit, Robinson spent his days in the ocean—the entire day. During the winter, he bathed the day away in an outdoor tub, having servants bring his meals there and conducting all the business of his estate while submerged to the neck in water.

●●●

Beatnik poet Joe Gould spent cold nights sleeping out in Greenwich Village, stuffing newspapers inside his suit for warmth. But Gould, a true bohemian, refused to use any paper for insulation but the *New York Times*, proclaiming himself to be a "snob at heart."

●●●

English eccentric Charles Waterton turned his estate into a bird sanctuary, but not for the kinds of birds most people keep as pets. Instead, he gave over the preserve to buzzards, carrion crows, and magpies, claiming they were the victims of discrimination.

Waterton slept on the floor of an empty room in his mansion, using a block of wood for his pillow.

He also had the odd habit of hiding from his houseguests, then jumping out to bite their ankles.

●●●

John Henry Patterson, the wealthy founder of National Cash Register, took four baths every day. He had his underwear made of the same felt they use for pool tables.

Jemmy Hirst was a great practitioner of the proper British hunt in the mid-1800s. Well, not quite proper. When Hirst went hunting, he eschewed the horse and hounds that other English gentlemen used. Instead, he rode upon a bull and used trained pigs to lead the chase.

•••

Edward VII, king of England, had one of those hobbies it's best to be king if you're going to have. He had servants record in ledgers the weight of every visitor to his castle.

•••

Jonathan Swift, who wrote *Gulliver's Travels*, developed his own odd way of traveling: He counted every footstep. That way, Swift knew how many steps his daily walks through the countryside would require.

•••

Saints often test themselves to prove their devotion to their mystical vision. Saint Francesca came up with the kind of test only someone on the saint track would not get rubber-roomed for—burning herself with hot bacon.

•••

When he was in the thick of his research, the English physicist Oliver Heaviside would live on nothing but bowls of milk. He kept warm while he worked in his drafty lab by bundling up in layers of blankets and wearing a tea cozy on his head instead of a hat.

In Liechtenstein farmers publish obituaries in the local paper when their cows die.

•••

The nineteenth-century earl of Aldborough, Benjamin Stratford, threw away his family fortune trying to build the world's largest balloon. His attempts burned up when his hangar caught fire.

The earl spent the last years of his life as a hotel recluse, having all meals sent to his room but refusing to allow maids to remove the trays afterward.

When he died, his room was piled from floor to ceiling with dirty dishes.

•••

Oxford professor Richard Porson was such a heavy drinker that he ruined his nose, the busted veins leading to ugly disfigurement. The professor cared nothing for appearances and could be seen walking around campus wearing a coat covered with cobwebs and a cone of paper pasted to his nose.

•••

John Bigg was a scholar and respected member of the judiciary during the reign of Charles I of England. Bigg had one quirk that set him apart from the rest of England's elite: sewing odd pieces of leather all over his clothes.

CHAPTER SIXTEEN

Fools for Love:
Tom Cruise Mows the Lawn;
Ivan the Terrible Solves Virginity

DO I BELIEVE in love at first sight? Almost exclusively. Second sight tends to make Hamlets of us all. Or Houdinis.

So who plays the fool for love? The volunteers, baby.

•••

When Edgar Allan Poe, the poet of gloom, was a boy, he showed his affection for the girls in his town by hiding in the bushes and throwing live snakes at them.

•••

An Iranian man who married 168 women attributed his romantic allure to his diet: two pounds of onions a day.

A survey found that 52 percent of American women would give up a year of their lives to have their ideal body.

The problem with such surveys is they don't ask: Which year of your life? People might give up their eighty-second year for a great body. But would they give up their twenty-eighth year?

●●●

Reason number 157 why you should never marry anyone from Hollywood: A society girl named Doris Lilly married movie director John Huston in a Mexican ceremony. Then she caught him cheating on her. She was even more surprised when he announced that he couldn't be cheating because they were never married.

Huston had talked one of the actors from his movie *Treasure of the Sierra Madre* into playing the minister at a fake wedding ceremony.

●●●

There are over one hundred romance novels published each month. That's more than the actual number of true romances.

●●●

A Bible printed in London in 1631 included an embarrassing typo. Instead of "Thou shalt not . . ." it read, "Thou shalt commit adultery."

There's one commandment that could be followed by people who couldn't follow the other nine.

Czar Ivan the Terrible announced that he would choose his bride from a lineup of one thousand virgins gathered from all over Russia. The decree proved surprisingly popular with the young men of Russia.

An unusual number of young women quickly gave their virginity to almost anyone else, in order to disqualify themselves before they could be summoned to the Kremlin for inspection.

●●●

Writer Charles Dickens had an endearing nickname for his wife: Dearest Darling Pig. She later divorced him.

●●●

The Indian potentate Gaikwar of Baroda was so romantically inclined that he spent $2 million on weddings. Not his own, not his kids', not his court's—he spent that much money on lavish weddings for his pets.

●●●

Can international relations actually be more romantic than romance itself? Few love notes compare to the one sent by Idi Amin, president of Uganda, to Julius Nyerere, president of Tanzania (a country Amin was planning to invade).

"I love you so much," Amin wrote, "that if you were a woman I would consider marrying you."

The invasion failed too.

You've got to have heart. Peter the Great, czar of Russia, kept the head of his favorite mistress in a jar by his bed.

But Peter the Great was not just nostalgic. He was also a jealous lover. When he suspected that his wife had a lover, he removed the paramour's head and forced his wife to keep it in a jar by *her* bed.

•••

Poets take a slightly different approach to love. When the poet Percy Bysshe Shelley died young, his romantic wife Mary wanted to keep his heart with her always, wrapped in a piece of silk. But they were poets, not anatomists, and Mary ended up with Percy's liver.

But who's to say the liver can't be as romantic as the heart?

•••

Not nearly so romantic was the German wife who divorced her husband on the grounds that he ate too much celery in bed and the constant crunching kept her awake.

•••

In 1946, an Ohio flag pole sitter and his fiancée got married while perched on top of a 176-foot pole. Like many marriages, it was a long way down from there.

•••

In nineteenth-century England, a visionary named Thomas Harris formed a religion called the Brotherhood of the New Life, under the theory that God was bisexual. To get close to God, followers had to get close to Father Harris, who particularly wanted to get close to young women.

Father Harris didn't do this for his own gratification, but because his bisexual counterpart in heaven was a spirit called the Lily Queen. She wanted to comfort followers of her own sex, which she could only do on Earth through the body of Father Harris.

"By getting into his arms," women adherents were told, "we get into her arms."

Enough people actually bought this line to keep Father Harris from getting lonely at night.

●●●

On his wedding night, Charles Joffe took his new bride to a performance by stand-up comedian Woody Allen. Joffe was Allen's manager at the time. Joffe's bride was dragged into the nightclub in her wedding gown.

●●●

When he was a Broadway producer, George M. Cohan fired a young actor from one of his shows because he had no romantic appeal. The dumped actor? Clark Gable.

●●●

Johnny Depp, in love with Winona Ryder, ordered up a "Winona Forever" tattoo. After they split, he had it changed to "Wino Forever."

Four Foolish Skirmishes in the Battle of the Sexes

1. "Love is the triumph of imagination over intelligence," said the unhappy-in-love author H. L. Mencken.

2. Writer Pearl Buck cautioned her daughters about the realities of married life with this estimation of men:

   "The bitterest creature under heaven is the wife who discovers that her husband's bravery is only bravado, that his strength is only a uniform, that his power is but a gun in the hands of a fool."

3. Anthropologist Margaret Mead may have been answering Pearl Buck when she said: "Women want mediocre men, and men are working hard to be as mediocre as possible."

4. "Girls have an unfair advantage over men," actor Yul Brynner countered. "If they can't get what they want by being smart, they can get it by being dumb."

In 1989, a boy asked a girl to their high school prom. Then on the big night, he stood her up.

The girl's mother sued the boy. What did she want in damages? $49.53. How high did that leave her daughter's self-esteem? First, she gets dumped. Then her own mother thinks she's not even worth an even fifty dollars.

•••

President Grover Cleveland waited until 1905 when he was out of the White House to embarrass himself with this remark: "Sensible and responsible women do not want to vote. The relative positions to be assumed by man and woman in the working out of our civilization were assigned long ago by a higher intelligence than ours."

Apparently, that higher intelligence found it necessary to work through such a lesser intelligence as Cleveland.

•••

Peek-a-boo-boo? In the early 1900s, upper-class English gentlemen hoarded naughty pictures of harem women from the Ottoman Empire, posed peeking out from behind their veils.

But since women in Turkey weren't allowed to pose for photos, many of these pictures were of men posing as women.

•••

What says love better than a fourteen-karat gold birthday present? That's what filmmaker Carlo Ponti gave his wife, the actress Sophia Loren, on her fortieth birthday. Romantic? Well, maybe. He gave her a solid gold toilet seat.

Just because you can do something to get into the Guinness Book of World Records doesn't mean you should.

Take Jack Moran, who was married forty times. So was Edna Moran. The Seattle couple married each other forty times starting in 1937, enacting repeat wedding ceremonies all over the world.

•••

When the artist Marcel Duchamp was married, he ignored his bride on their honeymoon and instead played chess. She countered by gluing the chess pieces to the board. He countered by divorcing her three weeks later.

•••

"You don't choose your best friend because they have a cute nose," writer Fran Lebowitz said. "But that's all you're doing when you get married."

•••

"I've never been an in-between type woman in romance," TV talk show host Kathie Lee Gifford said. "If I'm in love I want to get married. That's how stupid I am."

•••

When comic actor Poodles Hanneford got married, he wouldn't carry his bride across the threshold. Even though the practice is antiquated, she expected him to do his part. But Poodles explained, "I am an actor, not a porter."

The English writer Thomas Hardy loved his wife, Emma, so much that he requested to be buried next to her.

But Hardy, who wrote *Tess of the d'Urbervilles* and *Far from the Madding Crowd,* was considered a national treasure. So after he died on January 11, 1928, his body was interred in the Poet's Corner of Westminster Abbey.

But before the ceremony, his heart was removed, to be buried in Emma's grave. A touching gesture. However, before that could happen, Hardy's housekeeper placed his heart on a kitchen table and the cat ate it.

●●●

An unusual way of coming out. Here's how comedian Rosie O'Donnell let everyone know she is gay: "I never once said I want [Tom Cruise] naked in the bed doing the nasty. I want him to mow my lawn and get me a lemonade."

●●●

In Paris in the fifteenth century, a romantic-minded young man would take the girl of his heart for a dinner picnic at the public execution grounds. Which shows you the lengths people would go to for a date before they had movie theaters.

●●●

J. Edgar Hoover once fired an FBI agent because he married a woman of Arab heritage, which the head of the FBI declared to be an un-American romance.

In 1998, *People* magazine named actor Harrison Ford the "sexiest man alive." Ford was fifty-six at the time.

Apparently, all the editors at *People* were fifty-six, too. They assumed that in our youth-maniacal culture what most young women really want is to make love to an old man. Say, a fifty-six-year-old movie actor. Or if he's busy, a fifty-six-year-old magazine editor.

Unless, of course, *People* magazine meant sexy in the sense of let's run his picture on our cover and see if anyone will still buy it.

●●●

In seventh-century England, a man could legally divorce his wife for a wide range of misbehaviors, including being too friendly, too unfriendly, too hungry, too amorous, or too silly.

Who made the call? The husband, of course. His accusation was the divorce. It was that kind of world.

●●●

In eighteenth-century England, poor men who could not afford an expensive government divorce might choose to auction off a wife who proved unsatisfactory.

If he was a country man, he would put a halter around his wife and lead her to the auction block like cattle, then sell her to the highest bidder. It was still that kind of world.

CHAPTER SEVENTEEN

Rich but Stupid:
The Barefoot Explorer
and the Witch of Wall Street

IF YOU believe that rich people must be smart or they wouldn't have so much money, then you haven't met these wealthy ding-dongs.

•••

Russell Sage was one of the richest men in America in the 1800s. But when he saw his wife feeding peanuts to squirrels, he reprimanded her, insisting she feed them stale bread instead because it cost less.

Sage made millions—but never spent it. He lived in cheap lodgings and wore the cheapest of clothes. After he died, his widow spent the rest of her life giving his money to good causes. Ah, sweet charity revenge.

●●●

Billionaire Howard Hughes, during one of his more eccentric phases, lived for years on nothing but ice cream. Some of that ice cream he ate while in his private movie theater watching the film *Ice Station Zebra* more than one hundred times in a row.

People who didn't have a tenth of a tenth of his money couldn't make it through that movie once.

●●●

Enrico Caruso made a fortune singing opera all over the world. Yet his early poverty made him obsessive about spending any of his wealth. He wrote down every single expense, including food, clothes, and the smallest of tips in little black books, while stashing millions of dollars in the bank.

When Caruso died, he left behind hundreds of these account books, full of meaningless figures.

●●●

Millionaire Hetty Green, known as the Witch of Wall Street in the 1800s, was so cheap and senseless that when her son injured his leg, she refused to pay for medical care.

She told the boy there was no point in paying a doctor because he'd recover anyway. Her son's leg became infected with gangrene because the wound wasn't treated, and had to be amputated.

When you're poor, you have buddies. When you're rich, you have an entourage, and they can be so much fussier.

Movie star Jennifer Lopez took her entourage to London and put them up at a fancy hotel. One night they decided to go to another hotel for dinner.

It took six limousines and half an hour of sorting out who rode in which car before they could make the drive from the first hotel to the second—which was located one hundred yards down the street.

•••

The nineteenth-century Wendels were eccentric millionaires whose motto was "Buy, but never sell New York real estate."

In 1856, the family owned a five-story mansion on Fifth Avenue. They kept the grand entranceway boarded up, so everyone had to enter through the rear door.

Although they became one of the richest families in New York history, they didn't believe in electricity or automobiles. In the 1930s they still rode through New York in a horse-drawn carriage.

•••

John Wendel, the patriarch of the rich but cheap New York family, insisted that no business property he owned ever have signs on the buildings in case the signs "fall down and hurt someone."

He had an even odder reason for prohibiting wires connected to any of his buildings: "They might hurt a bird in flight."

The seven Wendel sisters refused to marry so no gold-digging men could steal their fortune.

Josephine Wendel lived in a country house where she entertained no visitors. Yet servants set places for six at the table every night. Josephine would move from seat to seat and conduct conversations for all her imaginary guests.

Another sister, Ella Wendel, had a French poodle named Tobey as her only companion. Tobey slept in a four-poster bed that was a precise replica of Ella's own bed, and he ate at a table covered with velvet cloths.

•••

Celestina Collins was a wealthy Englishwoman in the nineteenth century who had the odd habit of sharing her bed with three dozen hens, ducks, and other fowl. You can imagine how foul that practice became.

•••

A wealthy eighteenth-century Englishwoman, Lady Lewson, refused to bathe, thinking immersion led to illness. Instead, to preserve herself she coated her body daily with hog's lard. She lived for ninety years that way.

•••

Business magnate Andrew Carnegie spent $250,000 to establish the Simplified Spelling Board, which tried to convince everyone to change "tough" to "tuf," "trouble" to "troble" and "philosophy" to "filosofy."

Sir Harvey Elwes, a wealthy Englishman of the 1800s, was a miserly millionaire. He dined only on partridges, since he could shoot them for nothing on his vast estate.

During the cold English winter, Sir Harvey forbade a fire in his mansion. Instead, he walked endlessly up and down the halls to keep warm.

●●●

Sir Harvey's nephew, John Elwes, equally as rich, was equally as cheap. He walked everywhere through the London rain to save the price of a coach. He wore a wig a beggar had thrown away and kept wet clothes on all day, rather than spend money on a fire to dry them out.

Oddly enough, although Elwes refused to spend money on his own basic needs, he threw away fortunes gambling.

●●●

The Elweses were rivaled for stinginess among the English rich by Daniel Dancer, who would pick up stray dung off the road to use as fertilizer for his estate.

Dancer's dog was his favorite companion. But he broke the dog's teeth so he couldn't bite sheep because Dancer didn't want to pay local farmers compensation for any sheep the dog might injure.

Instead, Dancer spent his days searching the fields for old animal bones, which he broke into pieces so the half-toothed dog could eat them.

When money goes with fame, you can indulge childhood fantasies. Comedian Billy Crystal did, spending $400,000 to buy one of Mickey Mantle's used baseball gloves.

Other people may see the glove as a piece of old leather too worn to play ball with. But Crystal looked upon it as a $400,000 work of art.

●●●

In the eighteenth century, British Colonel George Hanger arranged for a strange ten-mile race between twenty turkeys and twenty geese. Although the colonel set the course and trained all the birds himself, he bet on the turkeys, which were trounced.

Colonel Hanger eventually lost all his money gambling and died in debt.

●●●

Abdul Hamid II, sultan of Turkey in the nineteenth century, was obsessed with defending himself against assassination attempts.

The sultan hired twelve architects to design different portions of his palace so none of them would know the complete floor plan. He filled the place with thousands of bodyguards and hundreds of trained parrots, which were to sound the alarm if anyone attacked.

To prevent assassins from poisoning his milk, the sultan placed a round-the-clock bodyguard on his cows. When forced to travel outside his fortress, he rode in an armored carriage and always kept one of his children on his lap to use as a shield.

Charles Waterton was born to a wealthy English family in the 1780s, but gave up his position in society to become an explorer and naturalist in South America. He explored the rainforest barefoot because that was the best way to climb trees.

In his eighties Waterton would amuse his friends by climbing high walls, then hopping along the top of the wall on one foot.

When Waterton wanted to study the vampire bat, he tried to lure them from their cave by sleeping barefoot in a hammock after bathing his toes in animal blood.

•••

Wealthy eighteenth-century Englishwoman Hannah Beswick was afraid she'd be buried before she was actually dead. So she left her doctor a small fortune if he would keep her body until he was positive she was dead.

The doctor kept her body, embalmed and stuffed inside his grandfather clock, for the rest of his life.

CHAPTER EIGHTEEN

Government by the Idiots:
How to Get Elected to Anything

SHOULD politicians have to pass an intelligence test before they can hold public office? Could they?

College professor Bergen Evans offered this view on the people who run our government: "Legislators who are of even average intelligence stand out among their colleagues. . . . For the most part our leaders are merely following out in front."

•••

Hi ho, Frankerino. In 1945, two popular show business figures were denounced in Congress for turning American youth into juvenile delinquents: Frank Sinatra and the Lone Ranger.

People say that if you don't like the way our government is run, why don't you do something about it?

Hey, complaining is doing something.

Then there's Canadian fisherman Russell Arundel, who declared a small island off the coast of Nova Scotia an independent country in 1949.

Arundel named himself Prince of Princes of the Principality of Outer Baldonia.

He wrote a bill of rights that applied only to fishermen, including the right "to lie and be believed" and freedom from "nagging and interruptions." The man had created a veritable utopia.

So all hail Outer Baldonia, the only nation in the world where lying is protected by a bill of rights.

In all other countries, lying is protected by the people in power.

•••

But Arundel isn't the only visionary to create his own country when he didn't like the one he was stuck in.

An Australian farmer named Leonard Casley got so mad at the government that in 1970 he seceded, declaring his farm a separate nation, the Province of Hutt River.

Casley found to his surprise that he made more money from selling T-shirts and Hutt River souvenirs than he did from farming. Come to think of it, maybe that doesn't come as a surprise to a farmer.

Twelve Stupid Things
the Federal Government
Spent Our Tax Money On

1. The Department of Agriculture decided that Americans needed to know how long it takes people to cook breakfast. So department officials funded a study for only $46,000 to find out what anyone who's ever cooked breakfast could have told them for $7.98 plus postage.

2. The National Institute on Alcohol Abuse spent a million dollars in the 1970s to discover if drunk fish are more aggressive than sober fish. Turns out they are, which is why you never want to go fishing after the fish have been drinking heavily.

3. You ever drive down a highway with a huge semi on your tail? The Federal Highway Administration wanted to find out how people felt about that. So the agency spent $222,000 to study "Motorist Attitudes Toward Large Trucks."

4. The National Science Foundation spent $84,000 on a study to find out why people fall in love. For $1.98 the Beatles could have told them that money can't buy you love.

5. Considering the typical expense of military testing, we should probably be thankful that it only cost the Air Force three thousand dollars to run a six-month system test back in 1979. What was the Air Force testing? How soldiers used umbrellas while in uniform.

6. In 1985, the Department of the Navy managed to snag a ten-foot doormat for only $792.

7. Your kids ever need braces? Fun, huh, and cheap? But you'll be happy to know that the money was well spent, which the National Institute of Dental Research proved in 1984 by funding a five-year study to determine the "effects of orthodontia on psychosocial functioning." Smile, it only cost half a million of your tax money.

8. In 1977, the Smithsonian Institution bankrolled development of a dictionary of Tzotzil, a language spoken by only 120,000 poor farmers in Southern Mexico, nearly none of whom could read or write—and, therefore, didn't have much use for a dictionary.

   If the government had simply given the farmers the $89,000 it spent on the dictionary they didn't need, they wouldn't have been so poor.

9. Next time you go on family vacation, you'll want to visit the famous Trenton, New Jersey, sewer that the Environmental Protection Agency preserved as a historical monument for only $1 million.

10. Why should Americans have to put up with the inconvenience of traveling all the way to the other side of the world to see the Great Wall of China simply because the ancient Chinese lacked the foresight to build the wall in a more convenient location?

    So in 1981, the Department of Commerce spent $200,000 to erect an 800-foot limestone replica of the Great Wall of China in Indiana, right where the Chinese should have built it all along.

11. In 1985, the National Institute of Neurological and Communicative Disorders invested $160,000 of the taxpayers' money on a study to find out whether you can jinx rivals by drawing X's on their chests. Somehow they missed out on the all-important XX and XXX jinx studies.

12. The federally funded National Endowment for the Humanities once spent $2,500 on a study to learn why people act rudely when they play tennis. They could have borrowed a racket, gone out to a tennis court in a public park, played a couple of sets for free, and found out for themselves.

Janet Napolitano won a close race to become governor of Arizona in 2002. Or did she?

A year after her election, the new Arizona phone book was published, listing her defeated opponent Matt Salmon as the new governor. What did the phone book company know that the voters didn't?

•••

In 2002 North Carolina Congressman Cass Ballenger came up with an original way to prove to critics that he wasn't a bigot: He had the lawn jockey in his front yard painted white.

•••

Tired of the same old Democrats and Republicans when you hit the voting booth on election day? You should have been around in 1952 when the Reverend Homer Tomlinson ran for the presidency on the Theocratic ticket, promising to substitute tithing for taxes and create a cabinet post of Secretary of Righteousness.

Tomlinson wasn't upset when he lost the election. He simply declared himself King of the World.

•••

English politicians are a bit different, which is how Screaming Lord Sutch came to run for Parliament from the Monster Raving Loony Party, on a campaign of improving Britain's climate by towing the entire island into the Mediterranean.

Three Politicians Who Could Have Been Comedians

1. President Ronald Reagan: "Now we are trying to get unemployment to go up, and I think we have succeeded."

2. Virginia Governor Douglas Wilder: "The first black president will be a politician who is black."

3. Vice President Dan Quayle: "Republicans understand the importance of bondage between parent and child."

Time and *Newsweek* have always been tough competitors, but sometimes you'd think the two news weeklies were put out by the same editorial staff.

On November 19, 1962, after Richard Nixon lost the race for governor of California, both magazines went on record as predicting the end of Nixon's political career.

Newsweek called Nixon a "political has-been." *Time* said that "barring a miracle" his political career was over.

Oops. Six years later, Nixon the "has-been" got his "miracle" and was elected president.

Here's how they get things done in Washington: The Dirksen Building was built in 1958 for senatorial offices. When the building was finished, they discovered that the floor was too slippery. So they covered it with carpet.

But the carpet was too thick, so the doors wouldn't close. So they took off all the doors and planed them down to fit the carpets they wouldn't have needed if they had put down the right floor in the first place.

●●●

Days before the 1936 election, a national poll predicted that the Republican candidate would swamp Franklin Roosevelt and take the White House.

Voters were rude enough to prove the poll wrong. FDR won the electoral vote 523 to 8.

How had the poll been so incredibly wrong? They took the poll by phone. Back in 1936, well-off Republicans owned phones; poorer Democrats did not.

●●●

So you say you want a government job? Do you have the imagination required for such demanding work? Take the Louis Nel test.

Nel was the deputy minister of information in the old South Africa. When called upon to defend the government against charges of censorship, Nel set a high standard for other government officials with this beaut: "We do not have censorship. What we have is a limitation on what newspapers can report."

In the old Soviet Union, it was illegal to play the game of Monopoly.

Scrabble was probably legal, but all triple word bonus scores had to be distributed equally among the collective players for the greater glory of the state.

•••

The Dutch government in the New World thought Peter Minuit had made a bad mistake when he bought the entire island of Manhattan for twenty-four dollars worth of trinkets.

The governors liked the island well enough. They just thought Minuit had been overcharged. Now you couldn't even buy a trinket in New York City for twenty-four dollars.

•••

Why was there no bodyguard protecting Abraham Lincoln at Ford's Theater the night he was shot?

We know his bodyguard went to the theater with the president, but after that there are two contradictory reports, neither of them a shining example of intelligent diligence.

Some witnesses claim that the bodyguard took a seat outside the presidential box and was watching the show when Lincoln was shot. The other theory is even worse— that the bodyguard went to a saloon for a drink and missed the whole thing.

Watch out if you enter into negotiations with the North Korean government.

American officials who've had that pleasure reported that North Korean envoys would sneak into the conference room each night and saw a quarter-inch off each leg of the American chairs. Why? So American negotiators would feel smaller and smaller as the talks proceeded.

●●●

Assistant Secretary of State under Reagan, Elliott Abrams gave lessons for a new generation of politicians on how to testify before Congress when he declared in 1987: "I never said I had no idea about most of the things you said I said I had no idea about."

Set that to music and we've got a hit.

●●●

Giving lessons to political campaigners everywhere was Virginia Senator John Warren, who proved you *could* make everyone happy during his race for reelection in 1990. Addressing the abortion issue, Warren declared that he was "pro-choice with limitations," but also "pro-life with exceptions."

●●●

Go down about a mile and make a left turn at the dead cat.

In 1987 when a dead cat was left in the middle of a road, the South Carolina Highway Department simply painted the yellow stripe over the cat. The road painters reasoned that dead cat removal was not part of their job description.

Why there will always be an LA: In 1990 Los Angeles Police Chief Daryl Gates suggested to the Senate Judicial Committee that people who used marijuana or cocaine for recreation "ought to be taken out and shot."

So we're pretty sure he was against decriminalization.

•••

Having a hard time deciding who gets your vote for president? Think about the advantages of electing a total failure for a change. How about a candidate who:

1. failed in business twice.
2. failed to get elected to Congress twice.
3. was twice beaten in Senate races.
4. then suffered a nervous breakdown. Then ran for vice president—and lost that race too.

Would you vote for a man like that? Thank God enough people did to elect Abraham Lincoln president.

•••

Adlai Stevenson, who ran for president twice and lost, said, "In America anyone can become president. That's one of the risks you take."

But who took the greater risk—the candidates or the electorate?

Thinking about running for office? Here's a winning strategy from political pundit Frank Dane: "Get all the fools on your side and you can be elected to anything."

•••

The brilliant English politician Benjamin Disraeli advised a new member of Parliament not to engage in debate during his first months in office. The new representative protested that his colleagues wouldn't understand why he refrained from speaking out on the issues.

"Better they should wonder why you do not speak, than why you do," Disraeli advised.

•••

When France conducted nuclear tests in the South Pacific in 1995, the French ambassador to New Zealand tried to calm everyone's concerns by explaining, "They aren't bombs. They're exploding artifacts."

•••

Does the following incident explain why we get the politicians we get? Or is it the reason politicians are able to hold so much power over our lives?

In 2003, President Bush gave a televised news conference that was topped in the ratings by a repeat of *America's Funniest Home Videos.*

Religion used to be the opiate of the people. Then opium was the opiate of the people. But nothing in history has melted more minds than bad TV, which is why television is so popular with advertisers and politicians.

•••

"The secret of the demagogue is to make himself as stupid as his audience so that they believe they are as clever as he," Austrian writer Karl Kraus explained.

•••

What should a president's duties include? Writer and occasional politician Gore Vidal had a suggestion: "The presidential ninnies should stick to throwing out baseballs and leave the important matters to serious people."

•••

In England, the Speaker of the House is not allowed to speak. Well, maybe that's not so dumb after all.

•••

A year before Bill Clinton was reelected president, the *Wall Street Journal* predicted that he would lose to "any Republican nominee who doesn't drool onstage."

That gives me great latitude to predict the winner of the next presidential race. After all, I can only do as bad as the *Wall Street Journal*.

So I predict that George W. Bush will lose to any Democratic nominee who is richer than the Bush family, is more popular with big business, has better connections in the Supreme Court, and doesn't drool onstage too often.

●●●

Speaking of candidates, here's radio commentator Rush Limbaugh on former Vice President Al Gore: "Idiot . . . liar . . . IQ of a pencil eraser."

●●●

In a 2002 election in the Czech Republic, Christian Democrats handed out free shots of brandy to voters. The Communist Party countered by hiring topless women to hand out their campaign literature.

●●●

Bookmakers around the country were so sure that Tom Dewey was going to beat Harry Truman in 1948 that they refused to take any bets on the presidential election.

Too bad gamblers couldn't get money down on Truman. The odds would have been so great against his winning the race that the payoff would have been enormous when he did win.

●●●

The Texas legislature is as rowdy as the state itself. In 1971, a representative named Tom Moore found a nasty way to show that the reps often had no idea of what they were voting on.

Moore proposed a resolution commending Albert de Salvo for "unconventional techniques involving population control."

The Texas House passed the resolution. De Salvo was the Boston Strangler.

•••

Speaking of Texas, newspaper columnist Molly Ivins reported that a state senator bragged, "If you took all the fools out of the legislature, it wouldn't be a representative body any more."

•••

Finally, we find an honest politician. In Senate hearings in 1989, Chic Hecht listed his qualification for becoming ambassador to the Bahamas: "I love golf and they have a lot of nice golf courses."

CHAPTER NINETEEN

Stupid Science:
Catapulting to the Moon and Beyond

"INVENTORS and men of genius have almost always been regarded as fools at the beginning (and very often at the end) of their careers," observed the Russian writer Fyodor Dostoevsky.

Of course, fools are also often regarded as fools, which makes it difficult to distinguish the ninnies from the geniuses.

But if these scientists studied the problem, I'm sure they'd come up with some interesting solutions.

•••

The U.S. space program spent $18 million on the *Mariner I* to get a close look at the planet Venus. Never made it. A few minutes into its flight, the unmanned *Mariner I* crashed into the Atlantic Ocean.

What malfunctioned? Nothing. The computer controlling the ship's takeoff did exactly what it was programmed to do.

But the programmer had left a minus sign off one of the directions, and that made all the difference.

●●●

Taking a different approach to space flight, the African nation of Zambia decided to send its own astronauts to the moon by using a catapult.

Zambian research scientists trained volunteers for the rigors of space flight by sealing them in an oil drum and rolling them down a hill.

●●●

Build it stupidly and they will come. The dumb architect who designed the tower of Pisa in the twelfth century built it wrong, laying a foundation too small to support the tower.

Year by year, century by century, the tower has been leaning toward falling over, despite the millions spent to correct the initial bad design.

But stupidity can have unexpected payoffs. Aside from that one dumb mistake, the Leaning Tower of Pisa is rather ordinary as medieval towers go. If it hadn't been built so badly in the first place, they would have torn it down long ago and the tower would never have become a famous historical landmark.

Women in ancient Egypt used an early form of birth control, a contraceptive potion that Egyptian chemists made from honey and crocodile droppings.

•••

American pesticide manufacturers wanted the EPA to relax standards on how much chemical residue could be left on food. So in 2003 they paid test subjects up to $1,500 to drink two pesticides (dichlorvos and aldicarb) each morning for eighteen days to find out if the poisons would ruin their health.

Both pesticides were listed as hazardous and considered possible carcinogens. Who would risk their health and lives for money that would provide no long-term solutions to their money problems? People desperately in need of quick cash, of course. Who would pay them? Scientists in need of ethics.

•••

Rock composer Frank Zappa had unconventional views on most things, including the universe.

"Some scientists claim that hydrogen, because it is so plentiful, is the basic building block of the universe," he said. "I dispute that. I say that there is more stupidity than hydrogen, and that is the basic building block of the universe."

•••

Nikola Tesla was another example of how genius and stupidity can work comfortably together. Tesla invented the alternating current motor, and his studies in electricity rivaled Edison's. Then he withdrew from human contact and became convinced that touching any round surface would lead to illness.

•••

Not all presidents need scientific advisors. Ronald Reagan, for example, found it more efficient to invent his own science.

Here's Reagan on the campaign trail dismissing the dangers of atomic energy: "All the waste in a year from a nuclear power plant can be stored under a desk."

That would have been one amazing desk, big enough to cover up the twenty-five tons of nuclear waste produced each year by an atomic power plant.

•••

Air pollution isn't a modern invention. The air in London was already so bad in the year 1306 that burning coal within city limits was punishable by death.

•••

Some things look moronic but aren't. For example, if you happened to be in London in 1898 you might have seen H. Cecil Booth sucking the dust from restaurant chairs with his mouth.

Booth wasn't a lunatic. He was an inventor, experimenting with the concept of suction. After his early oral experiments, Booth went on to invent the dust-sucking vacuum cleaner.

An epidemiologist wrote a scholarly article in the *Journal of the American Medical Association* about infections you could catch from the sport of mud wrestling. She recommended wrestling in Jell-O instead, doctor's orders.

•••

University of California researchers developed a health food drink that rejuvenated aging rats. Why anyone would want to improve the health of rats was not explained.

•••

In 2000 two computer drives turned up missing at Los Alamos National Laboratories. Call security—the drives contained vital secrets about our nuclear weapons program.

Never mind, call off security. Just found the drives. Someone dropped them behind a copy machine. Oops.

•••

The English scientist Sir Isaac Newton showed his genius early as a boy in the 1600s when he designed and built a windmill, sundials, paper kites with lanterns for flying at night, and a water clock with a revolutionary circular dial.

Despite all his early achievements, his mother declared that the boy should become a farmer. Fortunately for the world, he ignored his mother's wisdom.

Medical researcher Oliver Sacks reached this conclusion from his scientific studies: "Nature gropes and blunders and performs the cruelest acts. There is no steady advance upward. There is no design."

•••

When the seventeenth-century scientist Galileo supported Copernicus's theory that the sun was the center of our solar system, he ran up against church authorities, who insisted incorrectly that the earth was at the center of everything since they were on it.

When the Church denied Galileo permission to teach his theories, the scientist argued that it would be foolish if the "same God who has endowed us with senses, reason, and understanding does not permit us to use them."

Papal authorities banned astronomy and persecuted Galileo for years. He was convicted of heresy and imprisoned for maintaining what is now commonly taught in all schools.

•••

Interesting attempt at scientific reasoning by St. Thomas Aquinas in the thirteenth century: that the earth could not possibly rotate on its axis because a circular motion would be "violent and contrary to nature" and that "nothing violent is eternal."

In the 1800s, technicians made dentures from the teeth of dead people. The battlefield was a favored place to gather raw material. Often, the robbers didn't wait for dying soldiers to finish with this life before collecting their teeth.

In Europe, these plates became known as Waterloo dentures, while in America they were called Civil War teeth.

•••

John Dee was a sixteenth-century English scientist with a bent for mysticism, astrology, and wife swapping. His eccentric behavior didn't stop him from fooling most of England.

Before Dee died in 1608, he predicted that the world would end by flood on St. Patrick's Day, 1842.

On that day, two hundred years after Dee's death, English authorities were surprised to find thousands of people sitting in boats, loaded with supplies so they could outlast Dee's flood.

The next day, they all climbed out of their boats and went on with their lives.

•••

During the French Revolution, looters broke into the crypt of Louis XIV, the Sun King, and stole the dead monarch's heart.

Mysteriously, the royal heart came into the possession of an English mystic, the Reverend William Buckland, who had been experimenting with ways to achieve immortality.

Buckland reasoned that since kings were the select of God, he might assume some of that deistic favor by consuming the king. So he had Louis's embalmed heart sautéed and roasted, then served to him at Christmas dinner.

As far as we know, the reverend's experiment didn't work. Or if it did, William Buckland has been keeping quiet about it for several hundred years.

•••

Where racism and stupidity collide: Mississippi Senator Ted Bilbo came up with this pseudoscientific justification for discrimination in 1945: that the skull of a black person "ossifies by the time a Negro reaches maturity and they become unable to take in information."

Apparently, ossification of Bilbo's skull didn't prevent him from expounding baloney.

•••

Scientist and writer Arthur C. Clarke gets the last word here: "It has yet to be proven that intelligence has any survival value."

CHAPTER TWENTY

Dumb Predictions:
The End of Poverty, War,
and Chickens, as Predicted by
People Who Got It All Wrong

NEVER underestimate the ability of the experts to miss it entirely.

But clever experts can get it wrong and still maintain their status. Their secret? Never apologize. Move on. Say something else authoritative. Maybe you'll be right this time. After all, you can't be wrong about everything.

•••

Before he saved Britain in World War II, Prime Minister Winston Churchill took time out from his political career to make this farsighted prediction in *Popular Mechanics* magazine.

Before the year 2000, Churchill claimed, farmers would stop raising complete chickens. Churchill saw this old-fashioned approach to poultry farming as a waste of time. Instead, he predicted, farmers would grow chicken breasts and chicken wings without the rest of the bird.

•••

Check out this slick turnaround on a dumb prediction. Charles Russell, who founded the Jehovah's Witnesses, predicted that the faithful would find deliverance before 1914.

When 1914 came and went without deliverance, Russell simply came up with a new prediction: that the faithful would be delivered *after* 1914.

Smartest move an end-of-the-world predictor ever made was not to put an outside cap on the date.

•••

An optimist? Just a guy who doesn't have the facts.

But you'd have to be a raving optimist to keep up with auto maker Henry Ford.

In 1931 during the depths of the Great Depression, when widespread hunger and homelessness swept the country, Ford insisted, "These really are good times, but only a few know it."

Presumably, Ford meant the few, like himself, who had the sense to stash away millions.

Some thirty-five years after Henry Ford cured the Great Depression (well, at least his own), President Lyndon Johnson caught Ford fever and predicted: "It's going to be soon when nobody in this country is poor."

Maybe he meant soon in the big picture sense—you know, any millennium now we'll eliminate poverty.

●●●

Here's psychologist Kenneth Clark warning the country of a new evil in 1936: that people addicted to marijuana "lose all restraints, all inhibitions. They become bestial demoniacs, filled with the mad lust to kill."

Makes you wonder what he was smoking, doesn't it?

●●●

In 1914 Nicholas Butler, the president of Columbia University, made this call: "No civilized people will ever again permit its government to enter into a competitive armament race."

Oh, if he could see us now when nation after nation has built up their armaments to the point where the world could be destroyed a dozen times over on a bad Tuesday.

Or perhaps Butler was being sarcastic, in the Ghandian sense that no "civilized people" have engaged in an arms race because there are no civilized people.

Variety is an entertainment industry trade paper that reviews movies and plays not so much for quality as to evaluate the chances of box office success. That's why it's so much fun to see how wrong the pros can be. Let's look twice:

1. Variety attended the out-of-town opening of a new musical in 1964 and declared, "It seems clear that this is no smash hit, no blockbuster."

    The musical? *Fiddler on the Roof*, clearly one of the biggest Broadway blockbusters of all time.

2. "It will be gone by June," *Variety* predicted in 1955, referring to rock 'n' roll. Ah, but they didn't say *which* June.

•••

Here's a Universal Studios exec turning down the chance to sign a young actor in 1959: "You have a chip in your tooth, your Adam's apple sticks out too far, and you talk too slow." Guess who? Clint Eastwood.

•••

Hollywood rejected another actor for a role in a 1954 movie about politics, *The Best Man*, because he didn't have "the presidential look." The actor? Ronald Reagan.

•••

President Rutherford B. Hayes wasn't the only smart person who thought Alexander Graham Bell's new invention was useless. "That's an amazing invention, but who would ever want to use one of them?" the president asked of Bell's new telephone. Can't imagine, Mr. President.

Who else missed the significance of the invention that went on to connect the world and pester everyone with endlessly bad TV commercials? Western Union.

Bell offered to sell the telephone to the nation's telegraph company. But what was then our only communications giant turned him down. Western Union executives didn't think the phone would ever replace the telegraph.

Guess they needed a wake-up call. Unfortunately, there was no one to give them a wake-up call since they didn't have a phone.

•••

Ouch. David Lloyd George, former prime minister of England, dismissed the world's worries about Adolph Hitler in the days before the Nazis started World War II by predicting that "Germany is unable to wage war."

And even if the Germans managed to scrape together a few blitzkrieg units, we still had nothing to worry about, George assured the world, because "Germany has no desire to attack any country in Europe."

Oh, George, ever hear of Poland, France, Holland, England . . . ? Perhaps it would be simpler to list the countries Hitler *didn't* intend to attack, namely Germany.

•••

The strangest people can miss the strangest things. Here's the great Indian leader of passive resistance, Mohandas Gandhi, evaluating another political leader in 1940:

"He is showing an ability that is amazing, and he seems to be gaining his victories without much bloodshed," Gandhi said. "I do not consider Hitler to be as bad as he is depicted."

•••

Major George Eliot was an American military expert with a talent for shooting himself in the foot with predictions, the exact opposite of which tended to come true.

In 1938 Eliot predicted that "war between Japan and the United States is not within the realm of reasonable possibility."

Because Eliot was a recognized military expert, it must have reassured the nation when he declared that "a Japanese attack on Pearl Harbor is a strategic impossibility."

But Eliot was equally inept on two continents.

In 1939 he assured the Allies that "the chances of Germany making a quick job of overwhelming Poland are not good."

It took Germany only a month to crush all of Poland.

•••

As a producer of TV shows, Twentieth Century Fox has made millions. But the studio almost made nothing.

In 1946 Fox boss Darryl Zanuck dismissed the idea that television would ever become popular. He predicted that "people will soon get tired of staring at a plywood box every night."

What Zanuck missed was that when people get tired of staring at the boring box, they simply fall asleep in front of the set. TV is the adult babysitter.

Samuel Pepys was one of the arbiters of British society in the early 1600s. As such, he declared a new play "the most insipid, ridiculous play I ever saw in my life." What so upset him? Shakespeare's *A Midsummer Night's Dream*.

●●●

In 1956 comedian Jackie Gleason reassured a nation of worried parents that America would survive Elvis. "He can't last," Gleason said. "I tell you flatly, he can't last." And away you go, Jackie.

●●●

Critic Howard Thompson of the *New York Times* got it wrong twice in one sentence in 1968: "Of Robert De Niro and Jonathan Warden, the latter gives at least some evidence of a little talent."

Poor De Niro went on to become one of the great movie actors of his era, and did it all without talent. Jonathan who?

●●●

The producers who wanted to put *West Side Story* onstage for the first time needed financing. But they were turned down by every backer on Broadway.

The famed Broadway composing team of Richard Rodgers and Oscar Hammerstein advised the producers to give up the project because they'd never find enough young actors who could handle the difficult songs.

CHAPTER TWENTY-ONE

Dumb Sports:
Flying Pitchers and
Concrete Linebackers

WHEN YOU go looking for stupidity in sports, you don't have to start with the athletes.

Notre Dame football coach Norm Van Brocklin points us in the right direction by explaining, "If I ever needed a brain transplant, I'd choose a sportswriter because I'd want a brain that had never been used."

Now let's watch the players try to catch up.

●●●

During an Ohio State game, a football fan was unhappy with the plays sent in by coach Woody Hayes. So the fan yelled at Hayes's wife, "Your husband is a fathead."

Anne Hayes shrugged and nailed the fan with the perfect comeback: "What husband isn't?"

•••

One of baseball's greatest pitchers, Rube Waddell, was also one of the game's heaviest drinkers. During a booze bout on a road trip, Waddell announced to teammates that he could fly.

When they hooted him down, Rube yanked open a hotel window and jumped out.

He survived the fall. When he sobered up the next day, Waddell yelled at his roommate Ossie Schreck for not stopping him from pulling such a foolish stunt.

"Stop you?" Schreck countered. "Hell, I bet a hundred bucks you could do it."

•••

Philadelphia Phillies manager Danny Ozark said this about baseball, but it applies to all sports and most everything else too: "Half this game is 90 percent mental."

•••

To that endless list of dumb sports injuries, you'll want to add this one: Milwaukee Brewers first baseman Richie Sexson sprained his neck in 2003 spring training trying to put on a baseball hat that was too small for him.

Obviously, Sexson should have worked on his cap-adjustment technique with the team's cap coach before trying a maneuver that tricky.

And now back to the press box for this beaut: At a Super Bowl news conference in 2000, a reporter actually asked one of the St. Louis Ram players: "Is Ram a noun or a verb?" Noun on two.

●●●

Here's what can happen when an athlete and a writer get together to collaborate on a book. When he found out he was misquoted in his own autobiography, basketball great Charles Barkley said, "I should have read it."

●●●

Ever wonder why football coaches don't recruit at Mensa meetings? You don't want your linebackers thinking twice about going up against players like Jim Taylor of the Green Bay Packers, who explained his approach to running the ball: "I love to hear the sounds of breaking bones."

●●●

Croquet is not a contact sport. Plenty of people would say it's not a sport at all, but something to do in the backyard while the chicken's grilling.

Then there was the croquet fanatic George Bernard Shaw, the English playwright. In 1950 at the age of ninety-four, Shaw was playing croquet with friends when he threw a tantrum after muffing a shot. He kicked furiously at the ball, slipped, broke his hip, and died from the effects.

When baseball's greatest zany, Bill Veeck, ran the Milwaukee Brewers, he didn't give away caps and bats like other teams. Veeck gave his fans pigeons, horses, and huge blocks of ice.

"No, Charlie, just put the ice in your pocket. You can play with it when you get home."

When the city threw a banquet in his honor, Veeck showed up in a sports shirt because he hated formal attire. All the other men at the event wore tuxedos.

As Veeck accepted his trophy, he told the crowd, "This is the first time I ever saw 1,200 waiters for one customer."

●●●

Bronko Nagurski, the great fullback of the Chicago Bears in the 1930s, ran head down, plowing over defenders, often dragging them into the end zone—if they didn't have enough sense to let go.

He explained his unorthodox running style as an act of mercy. With his head down, he couldn't see the fear in the defense's eyes and be tempted to "melt with sympathy."

●●●

Jacob Ruppert Jr. was a rich New York brewery owner who bought the New York Yankees in the early 1900s even though he didn't know much about baseball.

Early one season with his team struggling to score runs, Ruppert misinterpreted the old baseball adage that in the spring the pitchers are ahead of the hitters.

"My players are all right," Ruppert expounded to a reporter. "You must understand that the pitchers are now ahead of the catchers."

●●●

Back to the great Bronko Nagurski and the time he ran so hard for a score at Wrigley Field that he crashed through the end zone into a brick wall. Nagurski knocked out a dozen bricks and rammed a hole in the wall. He kept playing while they sent in bricklayers to tend to the wall.

On another play, Bronko ran through the Redskin defense, bounced off the goal post, and slammed into a concrete wall.

When he got back to the Bears' bench, Nagurski said, "Gosh, that last guy sure hit me hard."

●●●

Baseball slugger Babe Ruth once got hungry during a game and gobbled down nine hot dogs, a couple sandwiches, and six bottles of pop, finishing off with an apple before taking the field for the next inning.

He got so sick that he had to be taken out of the game and rushed to the hospital, where Ruth lamented, "I knew I shouldn't have eaten that apple."

Maybe his teammate Waite Hoyt was right about the amazing Babe. "He came out of a tree," Hoyt theorized. "He wasn't human."

Plenty of baseball players are superstitious, but Babe Ruth carried his to an odd extreme. He felt that anyone he met on the street with a physical deformity would bring him good luck for the day's game. During the 1928 season, he hired a man with a humpback to cross his path before every game.

•••

Here's pro golfer Mark Calcavecchia explaining why he keeps an eye on the leader board while playing a tourney: "I like to know whether I don't need to do anything stupid, or whether I need to try to do something stupid."

Most golfers can relate to that sentiment.

•••

English racehorses in the seventeenth and eighteenth centuries were given odd names that would now sound loopy even to a horse.

Here are some of the favorites: Kiss in a Corner, Why Do You Slight Me, Turn About Tommy, Sweeter When Clothed, Watch Them and Catch Them, Jenny Come Bye Me, Jack Come Tickle Me, and the odds-on favorite, I Am Little Pity My Condition.

•••

Casey Stengel coached third for the Dodgers when they played in Brooklyn, but he couldn't get that group of misfits to play the game right.

One game Tony Cuccinello tried to stretch a double into a triple, but was called out at third when he ignored Stengel's signal to slide.

"I couldn't do it, Casey," Cuccinello explained as he trotted off the field. "I would have busted all the cigars in my pocket."

●●●

While warming up before a game, Brooklyn Dodger pitcher Frenchy Bordagaray beaned his own manager, Casey Stengel, then went on to pitch a great game.

Bordagaray then came up with an unusual piece of baseball strategy. "I think I can keep on winning," he told Casey, "if I can hit you on the head every day for luck."

Let's have a show of hands for people who would like to put that plan into effect with your own boss?

●●●

In Southern California, the 24-Hour Fitness Gym installed escalators from the parking lot to the gym so that you don't have to climb the fifteen steps to the front door.

Gym buffs can take the escalator, then go inside and climb on the Stair-Stepper so they can burn calories.

Here's a thought, gym rats: If you ran up and down those steps outside for an hour, you could get in a great workout and save the cost of a gym membership.

Three All-world Dumb Sports

1. Marathon slapping:

   In Kiev in 1931, two Russians went for the world endurance record in the obscure Soviet sport of slapping each other across the face. They hung on for thirty hours straight, and they weren't even mad at each other. At least not when they started.

2. Purring:

   In this Welsh game, a man grabs his opponent's shoulders and the two of them kick each other in the shins until one yells uncle. So why is it that the Welsh never conquered the world?

3. Long-distance crawling:

   A Texan named Hans Mullikin crawled two thousand miles from his home state to Washington, D.C. Why? Well, it has to beat purring.

Tris Speaker was one of baseball's greats, but he also managed the Cleveland Indians.

Speaker knew talent when he saw it. Except once, when he declared that Boston Red Sox pitcher Babe Ruth had "made a great mistake when he gave up pitching. Working once a week, he might have lasted a long time and become a great star."

Ruth, working every day, became a pretty fair hitter.

●●●

Back to the press box, where a writer will risk almost anything for a good line. Hornell (New York) *Evening Tribune* sportswriter Rob Roberts came up with a clever bit in 1990 when he ranted, "I'll push a peanut down Main Street with my nose if the Buffalo Bills make it to the Super Bowl."

That was Roberts you saw with the pavement nose later in the season when the Bills ruined his rant by getting all the way to the Super Bowl (before they lost). Roberts hung in there and paid off on his brag.

●●●

Athletes often experiment with strange training routines. But few of them are as strange as the way baseball player Walter Brodie got himself in shape for the 1896 season.

Each day during the off-season, Brodie rode a horse thirty miles, then wrestled with a trained bear. That season, his batting average dropped seventy points.

Our hero worship of great athletes has some flaky spinoffs. For one, a guy who looks like a star may try to pass himself off as the star, for free drinks or more nefarious cons.

One such impersonator had a tricky problem. Facially, he looked a lot like the great center for the Boston Celtics, Bill Russell. Only problem, Russell was nearly seven feet tall, and the look-alike was nine inches shorter.

The fake Russell explained to people he was trying to fool that he'd had shortening surgery so he could fit into his Mercedes.

●●●

You don't need to be dumb to be made a fool of, if you're green enough. When rookie Jim Wynn singled in a 1963 game, Mets first baseman Frank Thomas asked him if he'd mind stepping off the bag for a minute so he could "kick out the dust."

Being new to the bigs, Wynn did as he was asked by a veteran. He was promptly tagged out by Thomas, who had hidden the ball in his glove.

●●●

After the St. Louis Cards won the pennant in 1964, fans lined up early to get tickets to the World Series. The Cardinals fanatic first in line got his picture in the paper.

When his boss saw the picture, he fired the guy for cutting work with a phony excuse. Even worse, police saw the picture and arrested him on an outstanding warrant.

Three Smart Teams, Three Dumb Teams

1. **Football**
   Smart: San Francisco 49ers
   Dumb: Arizona Cardinals

2. **Basketball**
   Smart: LA Lakers
   Dumb: LA Clippers

3. **Baseball**
   Smart: New York Yankees despite George Steinbrenner
   Dumb: George Steinbrenner despite New York Yankees

President Gerald Ford was a big sports fan, in his own way. "I love sports," he said. "Whenever I can, I always watch the Detroit Tigers on radio."

•••

Perhaps the president knew this New Hampshire woman, who built a home on the edge of a golf course, then sued the country club for harassment because so many golf balls kept landing on her lawn.

Baseball umpires don't like smart-mouth players. So when Chicago Cub outfielder Dom Dallessandro gave George Magerkurth a hard time about his calls behind the plate, the ump told him to shut up or "I'll bite your head off."

The outfielder got the best of the umpire when he retorted, "You do and there'll be more brains in your guts than your skull."

•••

The World Bridge Federation tried to convince the International Olympic Committee to add bridge to the Winter Games in 2002. Why the Winter Olympics? Because the Summer Olympics already had too many sports.

But the rule says Winter Olympics sports must be played on snow or ice. That would make bridge far more interesting, to watch it played on a luge run.

•••

During a baseball game in 1880, catcher Miah Murray reached into the stands to made a terrific catch of a foul ball. The fans applauded, and Murray bowed. While he was bowing, the runner on first tagged up and went to second. The cheering continued, and so did Murray's grandstanding— as the base runner made it all the way home from first base, tagging up on a foul ball.

Not just anyone can run a baseball team. You need vision. Philadelphia Phillies manager Danny Ozark had that vision when he evaluated one of his players by saying, "Mike Andrews' limits are limitless."

●●●

More dumb sports injuries: A basketball player from Mississippi State slam-dunked a ball, only to have the ball bounce back and knock him unconscious.

●●●

Why boxer Mike Tyson could give lessons to the big boys of the WWF: In a challenge to the champ Lennox Lewis before their match, Tyson declared, "I want your heart. I want to eat your children."

Memo to Mike: Work on your right cross. In boxing there is no TKO by child consumption.

●●●

Owner of the Cincinnati Reds Marge Schott tried to bring her team good luck before a game by stuffing a lock of her dog's hair down the manager's pants.

●●●

Some fans go too far, and then there's comedian Roseanne Barr. In 1989 during game two of the World Series, she mooned everyone in the Oakland Coliseum. Showing true sports grit, the teams managed to finish the game.

When CBS broadcast golf tourneys in 2000, the network dubbed in the prerecorded sounds of birds chirping to achieve that outdoors special effect.

•••

Is fishing a sport? As comic Stephen Wright pointed out, "There is a fine line between fishing and standing on the shore like an idiot."

•••

Slowing down the competition in a sport based on speed? Hmm, odd idea. Yet, it happened to bike racing in 1934.

That's when the sport's ruling body, the Union Cycliste International, permanently banned recumbent bicycles from the sport. Why? Because riders in the chairlike recumbent bikes could go much faster than traditional bike racers.

•••

In 1791 Daniel Mendoza of London became the heavyweight boxing champion of England. But many people in the fight game disputed his title because he wouldn't brawl like all the other tough-guy fighters of the time.

Instead, Mendoza used a jab, footwork, and boxing strategy to win his fights. Many people in boxing considered those tactics cheating.

In 2002 Yankee outfielder Ruben Rivera stole teammate Derek Jeter's glove and bat out of his locker and sold them for $2,500 to a sports memorabilia store. At the time, Rivera was being paid a million dollars to play baseball.

•••

Finally, consider that sometimes you can do something really dumb and it pays off in odd ways.

When baseball slugger Mike Schmidt was five, he climbed a tree and grabbed a power line. The shock knocked him out and stopped his heart. But when he fell to the ground, the impact restarted his heart.

Years later, as a Phillies star, Schmidt said, "I've looked back and wondered why that stupid little kid didn't die. Maybe that's the reason I've always worked so hard, because I don't want to think that I wasted that chance."

CHAPTER TWENTY-TWO

The Power of Stupidity: You Only Break the Leg of the One You Love

WHAT DO people do when they're given too much power? Create human zoos, T.P. shortages, and the unanimous election.

•••

During the Franco-Prussian War in 1871, soldiers stole a thousand paintings by the great artist Camille Pissaro. The soldiers then destroyed the paintings by ripping the canvasses from their frames to create a dry path through a muddy field.

•••

In the sixteenth century, Russia's Ivan the Terrible killed an average of one thousand people a day. Statistically, think about how difficult that was for the czar to manage since he had no modern weapons of mass destruction.

And what if Ivan decided to take a Sunday off or a week at the seashore? A czar could fall behind and there would be hell to pay trying to catch up.

●●●

The world's first parking tickets were given out in Nineveh (now Iraq) over two thousand years ago to people who parked their chariots on the king's road.

The fine? Death by impalement. Tough meter maids back then.

●●●

The first zoo outside of China was kept by Aztec rulers in the 1500s. The zoo was made accessible to people with disabilities in a fashion that was different than the accommodations we maintain today.

People with deformities were kept caged in the zoo, treated as curiosities by the Aztec elite, just as they treated animals.

●●●

In the 1930s Hitler banned Mickey Mouse from Germany. So did Mussolini from Italy, and Stalin from the Soviet Union.

●●●

When J. Edgar Hoover was head of the FBI, no agents were allowed to walk on his shadow.

In a 2002 election, some 11 million Iraqis voted to keep Saddam Hussein as their leader for another seven years. Votes against Saddam? Zero.

In America ice cream couldn't win a unanimous vote.

"This is a unique manifestation of democracy which is superior to all other forms of democracies," one of Hussein's election officials explained.

•••

The condemnation of art by the ruling class is not a rabble-rousing tactic created by our own power-loopy politicians. People who think they know it all have been telling artists what to do for centuries.

In 1573 Italian painter Paolo Veronese was dragged before the Inquisition and accused of the crime of irreverence because his painting *The Last Supper* included characters that offended the Church: clowns, drunks and Protestants.

The artist's defense was amazingly modern. "I paint pictures as I see fit," he declared.

Surprisingly, he wasn't drawn and quartered for that remark. But the Church did order him to remove the offensive parts of the paintings.

Veronese sidestepped the authorities and lived to tell about it. He simply changed the title of the painting to *Feast in the House of Levi*. The Church couldn't object to drunks and Protestants in a painting about Jews because that's where they thought such outcasts belonged.

Three Megalomaniacal Rulers Competing for the Title of Your Royal Numskull

1. The Chinese Emperor Li Hsui assigned a personal bodyguard to each of his Pekinese. The emperor wasn't worried about dog assassins. He was afraid that bigger dogs would attack his precious little pets.

2. When Holy Roman Emperor Wenceslaus was fixed a bad meal, he had the cook roasted alive. Obviously, this is not the good King Wenceslaus everyone likes to sing about at Christmas time. Or is it?

3. If Queen Ranavalona of Madagascar saw people she knew in a dream, she summoned them to the palace the next morning and had them executed.

Some of the richest men in Europe in the early 1900s were the doubles employed to pretend to be munitions tycoon Sir Basil Zaharoff. While his doubles entertained at society gatherings in Monte Carlo or London, Zaharoff made millions by supplying arms to both sides in wars between Turkey and Greece, then Russia and Japan.

In World War I, he became a billionaire by selling guns and ammunition to all the countries involved.

The Zaharoff doubles did face one threat to their job security: Many of them were assassinated in Zaharoff's place.

●●●

Vlad III Dracula, Prince of Wallachia, was one of the inspirations for Brad Stoker's creation of Dracula the vampire.

The real Dracula (a Romanian word meaning "son of the devil") came up with a unique plan to eliminate poverty from his kingdom.

He invited all the poor people in his realm to a great feast. Then his soldiers nailed the doors and windows shut and set the feast hall on fire. All the poor people burned to death. No more poverty.

●●●

Frederick William I, King of Prussia in the 1700s, spent a fortune to maintain a regiment of giants, the Potsdam Giant Guards, recruited or shanghaied from around the world.

The giants, many of them over seven feet tall, were taught to march alongside the king's carriage and hold hands across the top.

Despite his fancy for giants, the king treated them so brutally that many mutinied or deserted. If they were captured, they were mutilated and thrown in prison.

At the same time that Shakespeare was enlightening the world, the powers that ruled England punished people for swearing by having their tongues torn out, branding them with irons, or executing them.

•••

Europe in the fifteenth century was a blood-soaked place, where the power-hungry were slaughtered by the power-mad. The three charismatic liberators of that warring century—France's Joan of Arc, Italy's Savonarola, and Bohemia's John Huss—were all burned to death by the establishment.

•••

From 1481 and for the next four hundred years, the Catholic Church promoted the auto-da-fé, a public mass burning of people accused of heresy (mostly people of other faiths).

Church leaders somehow missed the great irony that they were torturing and slaughtering thousands of people in the name of Christ, who was tortured and killed for preaching love, peace, and nonviolence.

•••

For centuries Catholics and Protestants tortured and slaughtered each other (and everyone else) in the name of the Prince of Peace. Much of this abuse stems from men of no understanding who lust for power and use religion as an excuse to destroy everyone in their way.

But what of women, kept powerless in so many societies? Take the role-switching case of Blanche Gamond, a French Huguenot of the seventeenth century, who was punished for her religious beliefs by other women.

Six devout Catholic women stripped Blanche, hung her from roof beams by her arms, then beat her senseless, taunting, "Now pray to your God."

Gamond was a mystic, who deemed it an honor to be whipped for Christ, so she was able to transmute her suffering into religious ecstasy.

This irked the women torturing her. "Double our blows," one woman cried, "she does not feel them."

Isn't that the same approach Roman authorities took when they crucified Jesus?

•••

One of Virginia's first congressmen, John Randolph, set a high standard for the behavior of politicians in the 1800s. If his congressional pages displeased Randolph, he struck them with his riding crop.

What nerve! Who did the Congressman think he was, a senator?

•••

William Randolph Hearst used his newspaper empire to attack Orson Welles's great film, *Citizen Kane*, which satirized Hearst as a power-mad tycoon.

Oddly enough, Hearst's influence was so strong in the 1940s that when *Citizen Kane* was nominated for eight Oscars, the film and the director were booed every time they were mentioned during the Academy Award ceremony.

The people shouting down what is now considered a masterpiece were not Hearst employees. They were Hollywood celebrities and studio tycoons, turning against one of their own to support the man who attacked their industry.

●●●

Johnny Carson, the country's most popular talk show host in the 1970s, once started a panic with a bad joke. On his late-night TV show, Carson claimed that toilet paper was "disappearing from the supermarket shelves."

It wasn't. There was no T.P. shortage. But viewers believed Carson instead of their own eyes.

The next day, there was a run on toilet paper in stores all over the country, as Carson's fans bought enough paper to last them for months.

By noon the shelves were emptied. It took three weeks for the overburdened T.P. manufacturers to replace everything that had been bought in the artificial panic.

CHAPTER TWENTY-THREE

Military Stupidity:
Why Generals Aren't in Jail

WHY IS it that people who miss it entirely are so often promoted to officers?

Haven't you heard of military tradition, soldier? Now shape up and go charge that hill. We're pretty sure the enemy is out of ammunition. And if you do make it back, we'll share some tales of really stupid military maneuvers.

•••

General Douglas MacArthur overstepped his authority during the Korean War and crossed President Harry Truman, who demanded his resignation.

"I didn't fire him because he was a dumb SOB," Truman

explained, "although he was. But that's not against the law for generals. If it was, half to three-quarters of them would be in jail."

●●●

When you look at the vast array of deadly weapons available to our military, you may think there is no need to invent more killing machines.

One of Europe's greatest military engineers agreed with that sentiment. He declared, "I will ignore all ideas for new works and engines of war, the invention of which has reached its limits and for whose improvement I see no further hope."

Who was that farsighted military genius? Julius Frontinius, a weapons designer who helped make Rome the leading military power in the first century A.D.

●●●

Field Marshall Leberecht von Blücher of Prussia helped defeat Napoleon at Waterloo. But off the battlefield he presented a problem to his allies. He was convinced that French spies were heating floors to burn his feet. So he walked on tiptoe anytime he went indoors.

●●●

While visiting Japan in 2002, President George W. Bush said in a speech, "For a century and a half now, America and Japan have formed one of the great and enduring alliances of modern times."

Kind of missed that whole World War II incident, didn't he?

Here's a lesson we can all learn from the U.S. Army: If at first you don't succeed, simply pretend that you have.

During the Normandy invasion in World War II, American generals planned to have the troops land on Omaha Beach, then advance behind bulldozers and tanks that would break through the German defensive fortifications.

But the tanks and bulldozers never made it to the beach. So the troops, taking heavy casualties from German fire, had to devise their own plan under fire. They eventually took the beach by outflanking the German defenders.

After the battle, the generals stood by their flawed strategy, even though it hadn't worked. They simply claimed that everything had gone according to plan.

•••

British scientist Geoffrey Pyke tried to sell the English high command on a bizarre plan to defeat the Nazis in World War II. He wanted to attack German-held oil fields by sending in a wave of St. Bernard dogs toting brandy kegs. The enemy would get drunk, then the English troops would attack.

•••

Not to be outdone by wacky British schemes, American military theoretician Louis Feiser devised a plan to defeat the Japanese in World War II by outfitting bats with tiny napalm bombs. The bats would then be dropped out of planes over Japan, where they would set fire to buildings.

Although the bat bombers never went into battle, the U.S. Army actually tested Feiser's theory. What happened? They burned down one of their own buildings.

●●●

In battle when you're not watching out for the enemy, you'd better watch out for your friends.

In World War II the first German soldier wasn't killed by the British, the French, or the Americans. He was killed by his allies, the Japanese, in China.

And the first American soldier wasn't killed by the enemy but by America's allies, the Russians, in Finland.

●●●

When they're looking for someone to help name a new military campaign, do they always recruit a guy whose parents named him Bozo?

In the Vietnam War, there was Rolling Thunder, the air campaign to bomb North Vietnam into submission. As that campaign failed, American soldiers started calling it Rolling Blunder.

Then there was Infinite Justice, George W. Bush's name for his campaign against Muslim terrorists. Problem was the name insulted all Muslims (including those Bush wanted as allies) because they saw it as a sign of religious bigotry.

The campaign was quickly changed to Enduring Freedom, which can also be read in a negative way—as in how much more of this American freedom must we endure, as they liberate us from our bodies by dropping bombs on our heads?

We may not be the world's policeman, but we're definitely the world's bankroll. Nobody can spend tax money on weird things like the U.S. Army. Except maybe the U.S. Air Force.

The Air Force got to wondering in 1990: Did the noise from its jets bother pregnant horses? They spent $100,000 of our tax money to fund a study to find out. The answer: a definite maybe.

•••

You should have been in the toilet-seat business in 1989, back before the business went down the tubes. That's when the Pentagon bought toilet seat covers for its cargo planes for two thousand dollars. Apiece.

They could have gotten them cheaper by flying a cargo plane down to the local Kmart.

•••

Just a bizarre coincidence, but when the Japanese attacked Pearl Harbor in 1941, the U.S. Navy command was known as CINCUS, pronounced just the way no Navy program should ever be pronounced.

•••

In 1990 the U.S. Army accommodated its powerful political friends by letting select civilians take target practice on Army ranges. Only cost us $5 million.

So maybe when the next war starts, the generals could send some of their country club pals over to fight it.

The Civil War began when the Confederates attacked Fort Sumter in South Carolina. Although the rebels poured in cannon fire for over a day, no one inside the fort was killed.

Then after the Union soldiers surrendered the fort, they fired a rifle volley in self-salute as they prepared to march out. That tribute killed one of their own men, the first man to die in the Civil War.

●●●

The first book in this stupid series documented the moronic atrocities of the French Revolution, where revolutionaries in their bloodlust to kill everyone else often managed to kill themselves.

But I left out the plight of Antoine Lavoisier, France's top scientist, who was executed by the revolutionaries as a common criminal.

His crime? Being a scientist.

Lavoisier took the guillotine philosophically, commenting that it "saves me from the inconvenience of old age."

●●●

During the Vietnam War, American GIs were equipped with the AR-15 rifle. The weapon performed so poorly that many American soldiers switched to using Soviet rifles captured from enemy troops.

●●●

When General Curtis LeMay was head of the Strategic Air Command during the Cold War, he described circumstances under which he would launch a preemptive atomic strike on the Soviet Union.

When reminded that preemptive strikes violated United States policy, LeMay dismissed the concern, saying, "It's not national policy, but it's my policy."

•••

The biggest blunder of World War II? How about the Japanese attack on Pearl Harbor on December 7, 1941?

Yes, the surprise attack decimated America's Pacific fleet. But it also led the United States to declare war on Japan.

If the Japanese had contented themselves with enslaving the smaller countries along the Pacific rim, the United States might have concentrated its efforts against the Germans and ignored the Japanese.

But Japanese military planners figured the United States was not strong enough to fight two major wars at the same time—in Europe and the Pacific. Oops, slight miscalculation there.

•••

Remember the Battle of Kiska during World War II? Probably not. Hollywood doesn't make movies about battles like this.

The Kiska offensive was an attempt by a combined U.S. and Canadian force to take the Aleutian Island from the Japanese.

Things went pretty well at first, as Navy ships shelled the island, then 35,000 Allied troops went ashore and took Kiska, only losing twenty-one men in the firefight.

Of course, casualties might have been higher except for one thing: There weren't any Japanese soldiers on the island. All the dead were brought down by friendly fire.

During World War II, when the Americans and British launched their counterattack with the Normandy invasion, German leaders gave the Allies time to advance off their beachheads because they didn't want to wake Hitler with bad news, knowing the führer's nasty temper.

•••

Every school kid (and lover of bad jokes) remembers that Hannibal crossed the Alps with elephants. But people forget that nearly all the elephants died on the arduous journey.

From this we learn that history rewards the survivors and the riders. Yet, Hannibal would be just another one of history's temporarily successful invaders if he hadn't chosen a unique, though equally temporary means of transportation. History also glorifies spectacular failures.

•••

In 2002 twenty British Royal Marines stormed a Spanish beach with assault rifles and mortars. When the practice invasion was over, the town policeman approached and explained to the Marines that the beach they meant to practice on was British-held Gibraltar, a few miles to the south.

A British Defense Ministry spokesman apologized for the mistake. "We were not trying to take Spain and have no plans to do so," he said.

The Roman Emperor Claudius II banned marriage in the year 270 because he believed that married men were too weak to be good warriors. They were always thinking of their wives and children, instead of marching out to die for the greater glory of Rome and Claudius.

●●●

The earl of Essex positioned his ships off the Azores in 1597 to trap a Spanish treasure fleet in a blockade. But at the last moment, the earl moved all his ships into new positions. The Spanish ships simply sailed right through the positions that the earl had abandoned and escaped the blockade.

●●●

The General Accounting Office found that Navy officers were using government credit cards for nonmilitary purposes in 2003. The officers purchased tickets to sporting events and financed trips to strip clubs, using money they charged to the cards at ATMs located inside the clubs. And these guys are planning our strategy to outwit the enemy?

●●●

During World War II, American fighter planes used tracer rounds to help the pilots aim at targets.

But it turned out that if the tracers hit the target, the deadly rounds that followed would actually miss because of differences in the ballistics.

Once pilots got rid of the tracers, they got rid of the enemy's advantage.

CHAPTER TWENTY-FOUR

The Beached Whale
at the Dumb-Off and
Other Random Acts of Idiocy

IF STUPIDITY defies intelligence, it can certainly defy classification. There is great creativity in stupidity because there are no limits, as we'll see in the tales below:

•••

After a woman moved to a small town, she called the mayor to complain about a DEER X-ING sign near her house. She explained that deer were being hit by trucks, and she wanted the deer to cross the road somewhere else where it was safer.

How much irony can you stand? A New York man sued the city for injuries when he tripped on a hole in the street.

Why was that ironic? The man worked for the city. It was his job to inspect the streets for holes.

●●●

Even Woodstock never had a rock festival like this one. In India every year the residents of two villages line up on either side of a river for the Stone Throwing Festival, which consists of people throwing stones at each other.

Here's a surprise: hundreds of rock throwers are injured each year.

●●●

In most large cities, out of every ten square miles, cars use four of them. The United States has more than 60,000 acres devoted to shopping malls.

●●●

For every real flamingo in the United States there are seven hundred plastic ones.

●●●

In 2003 an airline attendant alerted authorities to a possible terrorist plot when she opened a bottle of champagne and found no bubbles.

When the plane landed, the suspicious champagne was investigated by experts, who found: flat champagne.

Eleven Slang Terms for "Idiot"

Everyone sees everyone else as stupid—but not me, of course. That us/them view is manifest in the slang terms used by various professions when they talk about customers, civilians, and other people outside their inner circle.

1. TSTL is what nurses and doctors call a patient who is Too Stupid to Live. They call an obese patient who needs help getting out of bed a beached whale.

2. Tabloid editors call any movie star with an unusual personality a Hollyweirdo. What's a trained seal? An expert the tabs keep on file who will offer validation for any ridiculous claim going into the paper.

3. Stockbrokers call certain customers barefoot pilgrims. They're the ones who can be convinced to make investments that will pay off more in commission for the broker than profit for the investor. What do they call small investors? The little people.

4. Fashion designers refer to people who wear ugly clothes as butt soup.

5. Car dealers don't like people who shop for deals, so they call them fleas. What they like worse is a buyer with bad credit. Him, they call a roach.

6. When a funeral director has a customer who orders a simple cremation, without any of the profit-generating frills, that deal is referred to as a shake 'n' bake.

7. In restaurants customers who act like they don't go out to eat regularly are referred to by waiters as Clampetts, a derogatory term referring to the rubes from *The Beverly Hillbillies*.

8. Carnies call people who play carnival games they can't win marks. Townspeople are called rubes.

9. In Hollywood a badly written, unprofessional script is called an Iowa.

10. On TV game shows, the staff refers to the situation where all contestants get the answer wrong as a dumb-off. If they think a woman auditioning for the show is overdressed, they call her a hooker. Anyone with a personality that will look dull on the screen is called a Pasadena.

11. Radio talk-show hosts refer to boring callers as maggots.

In 1961 an obscure Canadian fad caught the fancy of college students in the United States: long-distance bed pushing. As a sport, it was like a combo of jogging and napping.

•••

Cambridge scholar Charles Ogden believed that the world would never live in peace until everyone spoke a common language. Toward that end he revised the English language until it contained only 850 words.

Nice try, but I'll bet we all know people (and not the same people) who get by with a vocabulary half that size.

•••

At a business conference, writer Clarence Kelland was asked to introduce a long list of speakers. "The obvious duty of a toastmaster is to be so infernally dull that the succeeding speakers will appear brilliant by contrast," he told the audience. "I've looked over this list, however, and I don't believe I can do it."

•••

In 1982 a New York dog named Lump Lump was given a "bark mitzvah" when he turned thirteen. Four hundred other dogs were invited to the Jewish ceremony.

•••

The small town of Gaston, South Carolina, finally gave in and set up its first stoplight in 1985. Two hours later, a car ran the town's only red light, causing a four-car pileup.

In 1801 an orchestra conductor tried to save the composer embarrassment by skipping much of the last movement of Beethoven's First Symphony. Why? Because the conductor was afraid "people would laugh."

•••

Everyone knew the *Titanic* sank in the frozen waters of the North Atlantic. But no one knew where the ship came to rest on the bottom of the ocean.

After several expeditions failed to find the *Titanic*, a search team in 1981 asked twenty-eight psychics to predict where the ship would turn up.

They were all wrong. So was the expedition. The *Titanic* was finally found without the help of psychics in 1985.

•••

Marysville, California, used to hold a town gambling event in which two 150-pound blocks of ice were set out in the sun, and gamblers bet on which one would melt first.

Hard to say whether this proves that gamblers will bet on anything, or that Marysville isn't likely to pass San Francisco as hot spot of the left coast.

•••

Radio newsman Robert St. John: "If there is a god, he must be looking down, shaking his head, and saying, 'What a mistake I made.'"

Four Dumb Epithets for Cities

Philadelphia got called the City of Brotherly Love because they named it before they knew better. But these cities got stuck with really lame names:

1. The City of Notions: Boston

2. The City of Spindles: Lowell, Massachusetts (because of its textile industry)

3. The City of the Violated Treaty: Limerick, Ireland

4. The Cream City: Milwaukee (because of its cream-colored brick houses)

When cars first came to Tennessee, the city of Memphis passed a statute that a woman could only drive if a man walked in front of the car and waved a red flag to warn pedestrians of approaching danger.

•••

When asked if whiskey made people able to perform tasks more effectively, Dr. William Osler explained, "No, it just makes them less ashamed of doing them badly."

When the treasures of King Tut went on an American tour, a New York City policeman who was assigned to guard the exhibit had a stroke. He sued, claiming he was another victim of the curse of King Tut.

•••

Lithuania started a new kind of pageant in 2002, a beauty contest to find Miss Captivity among the country's female inmates.

•••

Absentmindedness can happen to the best of minds.

When Oliver Wendell Holmes searched his pockets, he couldn't find his train ticket. The conductor assured the Supreme Court justice that he could mail in the ticket when he found it.

"The question is not, where is my ticket?" Holmes said, "but where am I supposed to be going?"

CHAPTER TWENTY-FIVE

Smart Thoughts About Stupidity

WHEN YOU start thinking about stupidity, you may agree with comedian Bill Cosby, who said, "A word to the wise ain't necessary. It's the stupid ones that need the advice."

Or choose your poison:

•••

Cartoonist Bill Watterson (creator of *Calvin and Hobbes*): "The surest sign that intelligent life exists elsewhere in the universe is that it has never tried to contact us."

Irish playwright Sean O'Casey: "All the world's a stage, and most of us are desperately unrehearsed."

•••

Writer Anatole France: "If fifty million people say a foolish thing, it is still a foolish thing."

•••

Anthropologist Desmond Morris: "We may prefer to think of ourselves as fallen angels, but in reality we are risen apes."

•••

Roman philosopher Epicurus in the third century B.C.: "Most men are in a coma when they are at rest and mad when they act."

•••

Philosopher Michel de Montaigne in 1580: "Man is certainly crazy. He could not make a mite, yet he makes gods by the dozens."

•••

Writer Rita Mae Brown: "If the world were a logical place, men would ride sidesaddle."

•••

Educator Laurence J. Peters: "Most hierarchies were established by men who now monopolize the upper levels, thus depriving women of their rightful share of opportunities to achieve incompetence."

Playwright George Bernard Shaw: "It is dangerous to be sincere unless you are also stupid."

●●●

Writer Gustave Flaubert: "To be stupid, selfish and have good health are three requirements for happiness, though if stupidity is lacking, all is lost."

●●●

Writer Harlan Ellison: "The two most abundant things in the universe are hydrogen and stupidity."

●●●

Philosopher Friedrich von Schiller: "With stupidity the gods themselves struggle in vain."

●●●

Philosopher Jean de LaBruyere: "There are only two ways by which to rise in this world—either by one's own industry or by the stupidity of others."

●●●

Attorney Barry LePatner: "Good judgment comes from experience, and experience comes from bad judgment."

Four Words of Wisdumb
for the Alternatively Brained

1. Look *as* you leap. Since you're not likely to make it anyway, at least you'll enjoy the view on the way down.

2. Every dog will have his day. Hopefully, they won't all be the same day.

3. You will catch more flies with honey than with vinegar. But what are you going to do with all those flies?

4. In these days when stupidity is a growth industry, you see fools all around you. Of course, everybody all around you sees fools all around them too.

Politician Georges Clemenceau: "America is the only nation in history which miraculously has gone directly from barbarism to degeneration without the usual interval of civilization."

•••

Playwright George Bernard Shaw: "I have defined the 100 percent American as 99 percent an idiot. And they just adore me."

Writer Jonathan Swift: "When a true genius appears in the world, you may know him by this sign: that all the dunces are in confederacy against him."

•••

Philosopher Georg Hegel: "We learn from history that we do not learn from history."

•••

Scientist J. Robert Oppenheimer: "The optimist thinks that this is the best of all possible worlds. The pessimist knows it."

•••

Writer James Thurber: "You can fool too many of the people too much of the time."

•••

Writer H. L. Mencken: "There's no underestimating the intelligence of the American public."

•••

Writer George Santayana: "The young man who has not wept is a savage, and the old man who will not laugh is a fool."

•••

Seventeenth-century scientist John Ray: "Learning makes the wise wiser and the fool more foolish."

Benjamin Franklin: "Wise men don't need advice. Fools won't take it."

•••

Inventor Charles P. Steinmetz: "No man really becomes a fool until he stops asking questions."

•••

Industrialist Henry Ford: "Thinking is the hardest work there is, which is probably the reason why so few engage in it."

•••

Psychologist R. D. Laing: "Insanity is a perfectly rational adjustment to an insane world."

•••

Hollywood mogul Samuel Goldwyn: "Anybody who goes to see a psychiatrist ought to have his head examined."

•••

Finally, two thoughts from that great thinker, Unknown:

1. "Artificial intelligence is no match for natural stupidity."
2. "The difference between genius and stupidity is that genius has its limits."

PART TWO

Where Did All This
Stupid Stuff Come From?

CHAPTER TWENTY-SIX

Ask Forty-five Stupid Questions, Get Forty-four Stupid Answers

1. Is life just one stupid, nasty, pointless thing after another?

No, of course not. Often, several stupid, nasty, pointless things can happen to you at the same time.

•••

2. What are the odds that we humans are the dumbest race in the universe?

With a universe as big as ours, the good news is that it's unlikely we're the single dumbest race in the whole joint.

Sure, it's possible. But the odds are on our side that when God scraped the bottom he didn't come up with us.

That honor probably belongs to an insignificant race in a backwater solar system that goes around praying to God on Sundays and killing each other Monday through Friday—and sometimes Saturday, depending if they didn't get the job done right during the week.

What is that prayer heard all over this not-the-dimmest fuzzy object in space? Thank you, Lord, for this incredible thing you gave us, life, and the brain to realize we're alive and that we owe it all to you.

Now just sit quietly for a few minutes because we have to go over there and kill all those people who must have gotten their lives and brains from someone else.

●●●

3. Do you think more people would be able to follow the ten commandments if they weren't so complicated? Like maybe God could simplify them next time around; condense them into one or two really important commandments.

Most people don't realize that the ten commandments *are* the *Reader's Digest* version of God's rules. Here's what actually happened when Moses tried to come down from the Mount with the ten commandments:

GOD: Oh, Moses.

MOSES: You talking to me?

GOD: You're the only one up here besides me, and I don't talk to myself.

MOSES: What now, God?

GOD: You forgot eleven through twenty.

MOSES: These stone tablets are pretty heavy, Lord. I could

take down forty, fifty commandments if you'd put them all on paper.

GOD: Like to, but you haven't invented paper yet.

MOSES: You're all-powerful, couldn't You move a few inventions up on the schedule? Paper would be nice. Some of those lightweight sandals with the cushion tread. I wouldn't object to ice cubes. This desert water doesn't taste so hot coming out hot all the time.

GOD: Moses, already you're forgetting the eleventh commandment: Thou shalt not whine.

MOSES : Right, right.

GOD: And number twelve: If you've got any questions about why life is the way it is, keep it to yourself.

MOSES: Right, because if You wanted to explain things You would have. It's not like this stuff slipped Your mind.

GOD: So Moses, take the next ten with you.

MOSES: Look, I'll come back for them. I promise. As soon as I can get people to follow the first ten.

GOD: Don't forget.

Moses forgot. Don't you make the same mistake. Write us today for a copy of the Forgotten Commandments, numbers eleven through twenty. Be sure to include a self-addressed return stone tablet.

•••

4. With the spread of nuclear weapons and other life-destroying technologies, is there any upside to the direction we're headed?

With our advance warning system, about thirty to forty

minutes before the end of all life as we know it, you'll have a chance for the sale of a lifetime.

90 percent off everything in stock. Everything. Everywhere.

Hardware, software, underwear. Salt and pepper shakers, popcorn makers, bread bakers, cruise missiles.

We mean everything. Buy one, get a thousand free, if you act now.

How can we make an offer this crazy? Because we're crazy. You know that.

•••

5. Can you judge a person's IQ by how much he recycles, so that the smarter you are the less garbage you produce?

Recycling demonstrates a psychological need to think we're solving another problem that can't be solved.

People have been producing garbage ever since they bought the odd notion that civilization was a goal instead of a collective personality defect.

Much of that ancient garbage is now treasured by museums as valuable artifacts of cultures past.

So don't feel guilty about tossing garbage. Think of it as helping some future Yale anthropologist get a cheap Ph.D.

Garbage: So what if it piles up? We have more important things to do. Waste is a terrible thing to mind.

•••

6. Have you ever met a dumb rocket scientist?

People are always saying, "You don't need to be a rocket scientist to figure *that* out."

Actually, there's only *one* job where you *do* have to be as smart as a rocket scientist—being a rocket scientist.

One more thought it doesn't take a rocket scientist to think: Whom do rocket scientists refer to when they want to be modest and imply that they're not as smart as someone else?

You don't have to be a supervisor of rocket scientists to figure that out.

•••

7. What's the world's biggest problem?

Overpopulation. And I could name names.

The solution is simple: Everyone in the world picks a number from a hat. All number fives have to go. That would free up a lot of apartments in New York City.

Where would they all go? Hey, I just solved overpopulation. Get someone else to work out the details.

•••

8. Can you ever win an argument with an idiot?

Let's say you maintain the radical opinion that "it's cold outside."

A philosopher might argue: "How do you define cold?"

A mystic would counter: "What do you mean by outside?"

A Democrat could contend: "If it was cold outside, the government would have alerted us to the danger."

But an idiot will argue: "You can't stay warm in the closet."

You might be tempted to say, "I wasn't talking about the closet."

Or: "Let's go outside and see if it's cold or not."

Or: "Even a moron can tell when it's cold."

None of these arguments will do you any good. The idiot will simply refute your logic with: "No, it's my closet and you can't play."

The only way to win an argument with an idiot is to think like an idiot, which isn't as hard as you might expect.

So the next time you want to prove to an idiot that it's cold outside, say: "Since no one knows for certain if the inside is part of the outside, all cold is relative to my uncle, and the government hasn't voted on the issue yet, let me in that closet now."

Then grab the idiot, throw him out, lock the door behind you, and consider yourself lucky to have won once in your life.

●●●

9. Are stupid people part of the problem or part of the solution?

Stupid people are our only hope. Consider pollution, which is getting worse day by day. But it's just not bad enough.

If our poisoned air and six or seven polluted oceans were really a problem, some genius would solve it.

No one's come up with a solution, so how bad can it be?

If you really want to do something about pollution, pitch in and make it worse. Let's not deprive some bright young scientist of the chance to win the Nobel prize for Really Great Science That Actually Does Something by solving pollution and saving what's left of the world.

Pollute as if your life depended on it because no pollution = no solution.

10. Free will or fate? Is it stupid to try to resolve that debate?

"You are who you are and there's nothing you can do about it," Phillip said. "You can't be who you're not."

"No, you are who you think you are," Megan said. "Until one day your thinking changes and you realize you only thought you were who you were."

"No, you are who you can get away with being," Rachel said. "Who you can convince other people you are. You can say you're a guru, but if no one follows you, then you're not."

"No, you are who we allow you to pretend to be," Chris said.

"Not true," Gabriel said. "You are only the illusion of who you are."

"Excuse me, folks. I hate to ruin the fun, but none of you are who you think you are. You are all who I thought you were."

"Hey, pal, who do you think you are?"

"The guy who thought you up in the first place."

"Maybe you only think you thought us up."

"I can prove it."

"How?"

"The same way God does. By stopping."

•••

11. Can we cure stupidity?

Sure, join the Society for the Unspecifically Unhappy or the National Organization to Make Sure We Haven't

Forgotten Anything by sending two thousand dollars to Post Office Box 2000, Needmoney, New Jersey.

These groups are devoted to curing stupidity by becoming rich enough not to care any more.

•••

12. If you are an idiot, what line of work should you go into?

Politics is always an attractive option. Our elected officials have already proven that any idiot can do the job. The trick is getting the job.

There's a lot of competition because of the graft and corruption. Also, there's no actual work to be done once you've mastered the handshake.

But for people just starting out in the idiot business, I recommend crime. It's America's largest growth industry. You don't have to be union to get work, and your competition tends to be even dumber than you are.

Best of all, there's job security. If you choose a career in bank robbing, for example, you don't have to worry that the bank will be sent overseas to be robbed for less by cheap foreign labor.

•••

13. If idiotology is a new field of study, how can you tell in which direction we're moving? Were people dumber before, and now are smartening up? Or were we smarter then, and now growing dumber day by day?

If people were dumber and are now getting smarter, then

idiotology wouldn't be a new field of study. Scientists would have stumbled upon it a long time ago because their primary observations concern the obvious.

●●●

14. Are there any advantages to being stupid?

Four, making it an attractive lifestyle choice.

1. You won't have to worry about losing your mind when you grow old if you lose it when you're young.

Good riddance to overrated straw anyway. The Scarecrow's brain never would have hurt if Dorothy had left him alone.

2. The progressive dumbing-down of America can be taken as a compliment. Everyone else is trying to become more like you.

And with the help of advertising and our government's policy of investing in smart bombs and dumb kids, they're going to make it. Meanwhile, you can sit around waiting for everyone to catch up.

3. Sarcasm relief. We are all bombarded by the cruel, thoughtless comments of miserable people.

You? Blithe. The snide comments and sarcastic barbs shot in your direction will fly right over your head. While other people have their feelings crushed, you'll go blithely on your way. Or would if you had any idea what "blithely" meant.

4. Greater range of food options. Butter-dipped pork rinds? You bet. Cereal made from sugarcoated sugar? Mmm, I'll have seconds. Extra cheese baked into the pizza box so you can eat the whole thing without having to figure out which is the pizza and which is the cardboard? Sounds good.

You'll never feel guilty for eating garbage once you go brainless. After all, if it were really bad for you, why would they be selling it?

•••

15. I read somewhere that April is the cruelest month. But I've never had any special problem with April. Is this a tax protest thing, or am I missing something?

April used to be the cruelest month back when they put a poet in charge of cruel accounting.

T. S. Eliot noticed that in April you not only have taxes, but also war, famine, illness, nasty accidents, and, on top of all that, the blues.

What Eliot failed to note, perhaps because his poetic license expired, was that right after April you get May, which also has war, famine, illness, accidents, and a deeper shade of blue. Plus, pile on top of that the remembrance of the cruelties of April, and you have a new leader in the cruelest month race.

Until June, when ditto occurs.

July? The same. August? See July.

The cruelty mounts month by month because none of these problems ever go away. Then you get to February, which not only has its fair share of misery and memories, but also takes on the whole problem of that extra *r*.

We all want to spell it as we call it: Febuary. But the English teacher who crawled inside our heads in fifth grade won't let go, and there's nothing crueler than that.

Then comes March, which luckily is the uncruelest

month because we know that no matter what terrible things happen to us in March, it's not going to be as bad as what's coming next: another April, which is the cruelest month, as the poet instructs us.

•••

16. Are the French and Japanese smarter than Americans because they teach their children to speak foreign languages at a young age and we don't?

They're supposed to be able to speak a foreign language. They're foreigners.

•••

17. Everyone knows by now that it's stupid to take drugs, unless you really love fried eggs. So why do so many people continue to do something so dumb?

We could have won the war on drugs by now if we had saved those Keystone Kops' billions we wasted chasing drug dealers from one side of the street to the other, and spent it on research to invent a better drug with fewer nasty side effects.

Those fried-egg drugs? Take out the drug reference and it makes just as much sense to say: These are your brains on TV. Here are your brains behind the wheel of an SUV. These are your brains after a really bad junior high school teacher got hold of them.

There's a world of fried brains out there, and they weren't all fried by drugs.

But you'll never wipe out a substance that makes people think they're having a good time even if they're not.

18. Is failure a sign of a subpar intelligence?

For too long people have been telling you that you're a failure just because you fail. Don't let all that negativity get you down.

Each year the Chicago Cubs fail to win the World Series. Do you think that gets them down? No, they bank their millions just like the champs, then go out the next year and fail all over again.

Failure is a humanitarian response. If you don't fail, someone else has to. Each time you fail, you give them a chance to succeed. You're a nice guy.

Remember, if at first you don't succeed, you may have found a lifestyle you can live with.

●●●

19. Who's dumber, crooks or lawyers?

Victims are. Because we allow these two groups to run our society when we could get rid of them both in one easy step.

We *can* eliminate crime in our lifetime. How? Make it all legal. Everything.

The way it is now, crime attracts the worst kind of people: criminals. No more crime, no more crooks.

Once we legalize crime, then everyone can do it. Crime will become as American as speeding or cheating on your taxes.

●●●

20. Do smart people throw away money more intelligently than stupid people?

Absolutely, as a recent study proved when researchers

examined the spending habits of people with and without IQs. They found that:

Stupid people buy: mood elevators, security systems, guns, subscriptions to *National Enquirer*.

Smart people buy: higher priced mood elevators, better security systems, larger guns, subscriptions to *Vanity Fair*.

•••

21. Why do magazines assume we're idiots?

It's a profitable assumption. Take *Vanity Fair*, a magazine for rich idiots, which ran an ad from what used to be Citibank but now is repositioning itself as Citi—a lifestyle choice instead of a place to open a checking account.

The ad advises us to "amass a fortune . . . in friends" because "they're the only ones who can tell you what you're worth."

Apparently, now that it's no longer a crass commercial bank, Citi is not bothering to keep track of your money. They're relying on your friends to do that.

In the photo, a woman is dressing as five pairs of hands tug at her white dress. Being rich in friends means never having to adjust your own clothes.

Or perhaps, the ten hands belong to Citi's nonbanking staff. Freed from having to waste their time keeping track of your money, the ex-bankers can help you with more important things, like looking good.

22. If we go into a war with God on our side, and they're fighting against us in the name of God, what's God to do?

Play defense. Can't you see that battle where God actually protects every mother's son and daughter by knocking aside all the bullets like some Super-Arnie?

They shoot at us, but they all miss. Then we shoot at them, but we all miss too.

It would get so frustrating to drill instructors everywhere, that right there it'd be worth it.

But then some general would order an old-fashioned bayonet charge. Now God really has to get to work. We stab at them and they sidestep, sidestep, sidestep. Then they try to club us with their blunderbuss butts, but we duck and weave like a pre-rope-a-dope Ali.

Finally, everyone gets so wiped out from all that missing they collapse in a big, nonlethal heap, and someone says, "Anyone got a beer?"

And the battle can't be won so the war has to end, and God goes, "Damn, why didn't I think of that before?"

●●●

23. Is it smarter to light a single candle or curse the darkness?

More people have been killed by candles than cursing.

You'd think people would remember to put the candles out before they catch the drapes on fire. But people are so busy patting themselves on the back for being so candle-lightingly optimistic that they forget to practice proper wax safety.

Meanwhile, people who curse the darkness are doing

their part to protect the environment, while developing command of a full variety of curses that will come in handy when things go really bad.

Take a close look at the universe. It's filled with more darkness than light. If God wanted the world to be heavy on light and light on cursing, He wouldn't have put so much space between so few stars.

•••

24. Why do the idiots always rise to the top?

They're handpicked by the top brass, who don't want someone smart coming in and making them look bad by comparison.

•••

25. Does watching TV make you stupid? Or do you have to be stupid first?

Studies show the average American watches seven hours of TV a day. That's not nearly enough. If you put your mind to it, you could double that.

If everyone watched TV fourteen hours a day, we'd cut our traffic jams in half. We'd also reduce the spread of sexually transmitted diseases because TV sex is the only safe sex. Tele-living is just like ordinary living, only safer.

•••

26. Why are smart people moaning and groaning all the time?

The more you whine about how stupid everything is, the longer God lets you live because He sees that you get it.

27. If you've already done the stupidest thing you'll ever do, isn't it all looking up from there?

Not quite. Nothing you can do is ever as stupid as it will become once your neighbor finds out about it.

●●●

28. Where have all the smart people gone?

Gone to flowers everyone.

Right off the top, we know they haven't gone to D.C. The last smart person in Washington was seen running from the Capitol screaming a warning: "They're not pod people."

If our government officials had come from outer space, that would explain a lot. But no, they come from America, and that's a scary thought. Apparently, this *is* the best we can do.

NYC, LA, Akron? No, no, no. If you were smart, would you live there?

You'll find most of the smart people in universities, where they hide out from the world because they've figured out what the rest of the world is like.

You'll also find wise guys in monasteries, where they seek enlightenment through reflection and meditation. And as soon as they find it, they make sure not to pass it on to the rest of us.

They realize if they showed other people how to become enlightened, the marketing boys would sell us Nirvana perfume so we can smell like heaven, and everyone would get caught up in the enlightenment rat race. There they may find a better breed of rat, but it's still a race.

29. Are artists geniuses? Or do they just get away with telling us they're geniuses because nobody knows anything about art?

All great art is motivated by one desire: not to have to work for a living.

Art does not require intelligence. If brains were any advantage to an artist, then Harvard MBAs would have painted the Sistine Chapel.

•••

30. Is it smarter to look before you leap or jump right in?

It's smart to look before you leap, but only if you look an hour and a half before you leap.

That way you will have plenty of time to come up with a good excuse for why you leaped after you looked and saw what you were leaping into.

•••

31. Are doctors as smart as they claim to be?

Experts estimate that one in fifty doctors is a fake, with no medical degree—and that doesn't count actors who play doctors on TV.

These impostors practice medicine anyway, some of them as effectively as real doctors.

Either we have some very smart impostors, or it's not as hard to be a doctor as the medical schools want us to believe.

32. Why are movie stars so fabulous until you actually meet them, when total jerkism seems to set in?

You'd be a jerk too if you were paid millions to romance a movie camera. Take Brad Hunk, your typical movie star.

Somehow he inspires millions of thirteen-year-old girls and suburban housewives to dream of the moment they stumble onto Brad at the mall, and he says, "You're the one I've been looking for all my life. All those Hollywood stars, the models, they mean nothing to me."

Yet Brad knows how inadequate he really is because a year ago he was folding shirts at the Gap. He doesn't know what he did right to deserve his incredible break or he would have done it after one day of working at the Gap.

Now Brad's a god walking the earth, worshipped by fans and managers. Every dumb thought he used to have is now a telling insight, written down by journalists who keep wondering why they didn't become movie producers instead of copying down the pronouncements of handsome idiots.

Brad now strides through the indefinite world with the confidence of a young prince surveying his father's harem. But even with the full resources of the beauty industry working on their behind, movie stars can never be good lovers because lovers merge with the other, and a movie star merges only with his box office.

●●●

33. What is the dumbest holiday?

In the spirit of Christmas, we go to overcrowded stores whose merchandising would have appalled Christ. We waste precious resources wrapping presents so the wrapping can be torn off and thrown away. We spend too much money for things we don't need and wonder why the holiday leaves us feeling empty.

On Easter and Halloween, we overdose our children with candy, knowing that within the hour we'll be yelling at them to stop tossing baby brother up against the wall to see if he sticks.

On Groundhog Day, we celebrate the ability of a rodent to predict the weather.

But clearly the favorite holiday of idiotologists everywhere is April Fools' Day, when we celebrate the fact that we are stupid enough to hold a celebration of how dumb we are.

●●●

34. Aren't phobias a sign of intelligence? There are things we should be afraid of, right?

You bet. People in power who have sharp implements in their hands. A politician is the last person in the world you'd want running with scissors, especially nuclear scissors.

But that's not what we're afraid of. We're afraid of spiders, our most common phobia, even though we're a thousand times bigger and a million times meaner than they are. When's the last time a spider swatted at you with a rolled-up newspaper?

More people are afraid of spiders than cancer, sociopaths, or being bored to death at pool parties by people in Speedos who have enough stomachs to outfit the whole neighborhood.

You're more likely to have a zonked-out rock 'n' roll singer fall on your head than to die of a spider bite.

35. They give out Nobel prizes for physics, chemistry, medicine, literature, economics, and peace. Doesn't that prove that we've got at least six smart people around here?

Prize winners are a small circle of friends, who take turns giving out prizes to each other, not to the rest of us.

They don't give out Nobel prizes for handicapping the football pool, channel surfing, whining, petty crimes, or living in a messy house—the things most of us are good at.

•••

36. Humans have invented hundreds of languages, all of them incredibly complex. Surely that proves intelligence?

No, but it makes talking a lot more fun. Language ability is more of a paradox than a sign of intelligence.

For example, when we want to tell someone that words fail us, we have to use words to get the idea across.

•••

37. Where do most idiots go, to heaven or hell?

Most everybody, smart or stupid, go to hell.

For starters, every religion condemns the foolish followers of every other religion. They can't all be right, although they could all be wrong.

Then there are the nonbelievers who are going to hell for not believing there's a hell to condemn other people to.

This leaves a couple of saints and a buddha or two with a shot at heaven.

But not to worry. Have fun. If you have fun and get sent

to hell for it, then you'll be with all the other people who got sent to hell for having fun—the party crowd.

The few people a century who stand a chance of getting into heaven will be honing their harp skills while perfecting pure thoughts. So guess who's going to throw the best party?

•••

38. Are ignorant people smarter than the highly educated?

We'll let you know as soon as the professors turn in their research.

Meanwhile, consider this: An ignorant farmer, walking through the woods at the edge of his farm, came upon a coiled rattler. Without thinking twice, the farmer raised his shotgun and killed the snake before it could strike.

Loss of the snake subtly shifted the area's ecological makeup. Without the rattlesnake, the population of wood rats increased rapidly.

Searching for food, the rats invaded the farm, bringing with them a disease that killed the farmer's chickens.

He treated the survivors with a chemical that saved some chickens but seeped into the soil, where it destroyed his corn harvest. Without a cash crop, the farmer couldn't pay his mortgage and lost the farm.

Fed up with his ineptitude, the farmer's wife ran off with an Indian snake charmer.

Despondent and completely clueless as to why life was so unfair, the ex-farmer wandered into the big city, where he became a street-corner drunk. He was killed in a knife fight over a bottle of cheap whiskey outside a skid row bar called the Snake Bite.

A few hundred miles away, an educated farmer with a Ph.D. in organic interdependency was walking through the woods at the edge of his farm when he came across a coiled rattlesnake.

As he raised his shotgun, the educated farmer thought about the consequences of killing the snake: how it might upset the delicate ecological balance he'd carefully nurtured. Further, his presumptive shooting would be unfair to snakes and other living creatures. Plus, it might come back to bite him at harvest time with increased vermin population and other problems that a snakeless ecology could introduce to the art of sensitive cultivation.

While the educated farmer was projecting these consequences in a nonlinear fashion, the snake struck and killed him.

There, I hope that answers your question.

●●●

39. Since the experts so often turn out to be wrong, shouldn't we be getting smarter experts?

Planes crash. Ships sink. Rockets explode. The power goes out. The toast burns.

We train the best soldiers in the world, give them the finest equipment, then send them out on impossible missions and they fail. That's why the mission was impossible, as the generals conclude in their follow-up report.

It takes a wise man to admit that he's wrong. Therefore, a wise man could never be an expert.

40. If primitive people were so smart, why did they create us?

They had a sense of humor before they knew that there was anything to laugh at.

If civilization manages to self-destruct, we will have achieved an irony none of us will be around to appreciate—thereby creating no irony at all, how ironic—by turning civilized people back into primitive people once again.

•••

41. Isn't marriage just another form of marketing?

Genuine marriage: Doesn't taste as good as passion, but it's less filling.

There's always money to be made from any product that can be improved by words like *genuine* (beer) or *true* (love). But the money will be made by the people who service the product, not by the people who consume it.

•••

42. Is there a new dumb trend coming into fashion?

Tough question, since all fashion trends are dumb. But watch out for extend marketing. For example, women will soon be buying giant tubes of bodystick because lipstick is not just for lips any more.

Why should your mouth get all the attention? Isn't your neck kissable? How dare they ignore the inside of your wrist?

Now through the magic of bodystick you can send out signals of where you'd like to be kissed next.

43. Is mankind too dumb to live?

No, we survive because of our ferocious stupidity. Only idiots would live in endless warfare that kills millions of people.

Yet, without all our wars, the planet would be jammed with millions of more people and where would we put them? Underground was a stupid solution, but effective.

•••

44. In the first stupid book you said the future was looking pretty dumb. Now it is that future. So were you right or what?

You make the call—although if you're smart enough to do that you're probably too smart to do it.

First, count the wars, the oppression, random cruelty, the way wealth taunts poverty, the continuing destruction of the only world we've got.

Everybody knows we're screwing up big time. Nobody stops. But hey, the president's happy we're still shopping.

•••

45. Any hope for the future?

Has to be. You can't have hope for the past.

The future was invented so we'd have someplace to put all the hope that keeps springing eternal.

You ever notice how hope always springs? It doesn't slip or sashay or walk calmly to the nearest exit.

Hope has to spring because if it doesn't take a flying leap, it's not going anywhere.

CHAPTER TWENTY-SEVEN

Twenty-one Stupid Solutions to Problems You Didn't Even Know We Had

1. Bad money

I have nothing against old presidents who are no longer with us, but if they're no longer with us and we didn't know them personally, why do we keep their pictures in our pockets?

Wouldn't it make more cents to sell that space off to corporations? They've got most of our money anyway. So why shouldn't they pay for the naming rights?

- Disney would sponsor the one-dollar bill because that's a Mickey Mouse denomination anyway.

- The twenty-dollar bill, built Ford tough.

- The MasterCard fifty-dollar bill: You'll never get one of these with American Express.

- The quarter? Mickey D's. Just get rid of the eagle and imprint the coin with the Macdonald's quarter pounder with cheese.

- The dime? Sponsored by Wal-Mart, only now it's marked down to six and a half cents.

●●●

2. Car cheats

Most people feel dumb when they buy a car. You could switch to riding a bicycle. Okay, but seriously, there is a way to get over feeling cheated.

Just follow this advice from the National Association of Concerned Car Salesmen: If we sell you a lemon, shut up and make lemonade, you pathetic loser.

Sure, our cars are lousy. You think you can make them any better, you're welcome to come down and try.

Maybe they do break down at the most inconvenient moment. So what? That's life, in case you haven't noticed.

You can whine about it, or you can look at that leaky radiator as half full, an opportunity to better yourself.

Do you realize you'll burn off 890 calories just by pushing one of our lemons into the repair shop? And the more time your car spends in the shop, the less air pollution your kids have to breathe. We're doing our part to clean up American air with American-built cars.

Making something that works most of the time is job one. Advertising is job two, three, four, five. All right, and one, too.

3. Unwanted senility

Social security will shortchange you in your old age. And you don't want to end an occasionally dignified life eating cat food and sitting at bus stops pretending you have someplace to go.

But now we can make lingering illness and debilitating diseases a thing of the past.

How? By stopping the senseless slaughter of our young soldiers—and subbing in the senseless slaughter of very old soldiers.

Let's not send our sons and daughters around the world to kill other people. Let's send our grandparents.

War: the lasting solution to the problems of old age, coming soon to a disputed territory near you.

•••

4. Unhappy fat

Fat people are looked down upon as dumb by skinny people. But really, they're just differently weighted.

Skinny people are from Pluto. Fat people are from Jupiter.

Skinny people get all the good press because photo editors pull the strings.

If supersized people launched their own PR campaign, it would go something like this:

We're fat. The way people were meant to be. Can't see your toes? We've seen them, and believe us you don't want to.

So have seconds. Do your part to fight the international diet conspiracy of skinny losers who are afraid to live large, or extralarge.

We're not twice as big as they are. We're twice as good.

So eat up. The more of you there is, the less room there is for them.

•••

5. Ugly no more

People who buy *People* tend to associate intelligence with good looks. Is there any real connection?

Sure, if you're beautiful—smart move. And call, we'll do after-lunch.

But if you're ugly and dumb, at last there's a solution, and it comes from an unexpected source. Listen in:

"Say Marge, I couldn't help but notice . . ."

"What, Sally?"

"You're really ugly, Marge."

"I know, Sally, but what can I do about it?"

"Haven't you heard? Avis has a wonderful new program that can help ugly people like you."

"Sounds too good to be true. How does it work?"

"Simple. All the really ugly people . . ."

"You mean like me?"

"That's right, Marge. All the real clock stoppers move to New Jersey."

"Hmmm. Why New Jersey?"

"Remember when we had all the gun nuts move to Montana? Same principle."

"Makes sense to me, Sally. Ugly people go to Jersey."

"You'll feel more at home with your own kind, and the rest of us won't get nauseous."

So remember, beauty (like intelligence) may only be skin deep. But that's as far as anyone looks.

•••

6. Beating the market

Every system for picking winners on the stock market turns out to be a loser. But now there is an investment plan that won't make you feel like an idiot.

It's manic depression: the investment strategy for the post-Enron years.

How does it work? Simple: Buy when you're low. Sell when you're high.

Any psychiatrist can cure manic depression. We'll show you how to turn your up-and-down cycle into a moneymaker, because nothing reflects your own violent mood swings like the stock market.

Our system will make you rich, then poor, then rich again. If you're manic-depressive, or would like to be, you may never find mental stability. But you can achieve financial security. And who needs sanity when you're rich?

•••

7. Guaranteed love

They say any fool can fall in love. What about a complete idiot? Is there really someone out there for every dunderhead?

Yes, it no longer matters how dumb you are because every day your chances of finding true love get better and better.

Odds used to be a million to one you'd never find the

perfect mate. But as the world population grows, those odds keep improving in your favor.

The secret to true love is that you've been looking in all the wrong places. Stop searching for romance in Beverly Hills and Palm Beach. Those beautiful people are all taken.

Look for your perfect mate where the love professionals look: China, India, the Bronx. There's a reason these are the most overpopulated countries in the world. They're full of young lovers, looking for someone just like you.

As an idiot, you'll understand that overpopulation isn't a problem threatening to destroy the world's resources and bankrupt the planet. It's all about romance.

How can there ever be too many lovers in the world?

•••

8. Republican air

Every time we elect Republicans, our environment goes to hell. Is this a coincidence?

Studies show that only 67 percent of the air is actually poisoned by pollution. Simple Republican math will tell you that means 32 percent of the air is good, old-fashioned American oxygen.

And because the Republicans are in charge, all that good air remains absolutely free to everyone, regardless of race, religion, or lung power.

Ask yourself: What have the Democrats done for your cardiovascular system lately?

The challenge for right-thinking Americans is how to get hold of that good 32 percent and send the bad air to developing countries, where it doesn't matter what they breathe because they don't have any Republicans over there.

The answer is the Republican Sniff. You probably thought we had our noses in the air because we were snobs. Nothing could be further from the truth.

The Republican Sniff is the only way to search out that 32 percent of the air that's still breathable.

So you can sit there and breathe the old, tired Democratic way. Or you can join us and breathe free again.

Air: brought to you by the Republican Party. And they say we never gave you anything.

●●●

9. Don't just say no

If all the people who just say no to drugs have been just saying no for so many years, how come we still have so many drugs?

Because just saying no to drugs is a stupid answer, when you could say so much more.

With our home-study program, you'll learn to say nay, nix, nope, nowise, noways, by no means, by no manner of means, on no account, in no respect, not in the least, not by a long shot, and not by a long chalk to drugs.

Now that'll get dealers to sit up and listen.

Let's face it—half the people who just say no to drugs are high when they say it. Why not put that time to better use?

With our vocabulary enrichment course, you won't just be lying around in a drug-induced stupor. You'll be lying around in a drug-induced stupor *and* improving your word power at the same time.

Our thesaurus is designed specifically for people who are too stoned to look anything up. We don't arrange words alphabetically or by subject, like those straight word finders. Our book has no order whatsoever. So you'll feel right at home wandering aimlessly through the absurd pages and improving your mind at the same time.

When your parents complain, "Why are you wasting your life getting high?" you can reply, "I'm not wasting my life. I'm dissipating my existence."

We've turned thousands of drunks into inebriates and fifty-seven junkies into alternative consciousness facilitators. We can do the same for you. Word power to the people!

●●●

10. That fifth doctor

You know those TV commercials where four out of five doctors agree? Ever wonder: What if the fifth doctor is the smart one, and the other four are like the idiots you go to?

The American Mediocre Medical Association offers this advice: four out of five doctors agree—stop whining.

Headache? Muscle ache? Where have you been, pal? That's nothing compared to the alternatives.

You could have phlebitis, phlebutus, or even phlebootius. Your hair could be falling out in clumps. So could your toes. Spinal chord leakage. Brain seepage. Intestinal gnats. And that's just off the top of our heads.

So when you have minor headache or backache pain, or hear "Achy Breaky Heart" on golden oldies radio, doctors recommend you keep it to yourself. No one wants to hear your petty problems all day long.

Take two aspirin. Take four. Who cares? Just don't call us in the morning.

The Only Doctors You'll Ever Be Able to Go to Association: From now on, nothing but the truth.

•••

11. Driven gay

In every car commercial on TV, sexy women are always turning to ogle any guy in a new car. Think about how many awkwardly dumb problems this creates for gay guys.

Homosexual men in good cars who are besieged by the unwanted advances of gorgeous women need a car of their own—the Gay Car.

You're not like other men. Why should you drive their cars? When you slip behind the wheel of a Gay Car, women will move back to Tulsa, Oklahoma.

What else can they do when you're driving the Gay Car, the only car ever made that will never drive women crazy?

•••

12. Leftover idiots

At last there's help for the idiots left out of all those other idiot guidebooks. Here are two excerpts from *The Stupid Idiot's Dumb Guide to Moronic Career Success.*

1. So you want to be a bank robber?

They'll give you the money, no problem. Don't even need a gun. Just tell them you have one. We guarantee they won't say, "Can you pull it out and shoot someone, please, to prove you mean it?"

Crowd control inside the bank—that's your problem. Most people who use banks will experience unnecessary anxiety when looking down the barrel of a gun. It's your job to calm them down.

Instead of threatening to shoot everyone, pass out peanuts and diet sodas. Then they'll do anything you tell them. Hey, it works for the airlines.

2. Thinking about a career in drugs?

You don't want to waste all your time getting deadbeat clients to pay their bills. Most dealers simply sell to the wrong demographic. Drug users make lousy customers because they're so stoned they can't keep their business straight.

Who should you sell to? Members of the Rotary and Kiwanis clubs, upstanding citizens who always pay their bills on time.

●●●

13. Happy money

You've probably heard that money can't buy happiness. Rich people have been telling that one to poor people for generations.

The truth is money can't buy *you* happiness, but it's done pretty well by us.

Of course, the life of the wealthy isn't all fun and games.

All right, it is all fun and games. But we're used to it. You wouldn't like it. Being rich isn't for everyone.

Do you have any idea how dreary those banquets can be? Resort, resort, resort—please.

The yacht? A constant headache. If it's not the helicopter pad that needs polishing, it's the crew jumping ship in the Bahamas. And you can never keep sand out of the carpets. Jet lag? You don't want to know.

Rich people. We're not better than you are. . . . All right, we are.

●●●

14. Phones for boneheads

Every night we get phone calls from phone companies offering us new phone services. You may ask them, "You got a phone service that prevents phone companies from calling me up?" They don't.

But at last there's a company that's less stupid than all the rest. The phone service from Ma Tell-and-Tell.

Other outfits offer cheaper rates and better service. But only Ma Tell-and-Tell gives you what the other phone companies can't: something to talk about.

When you sign up, they'll let you in on some of the hottest gossip in show business, sports, politics, and other celebrity rackets.

Like which eighty-eight-pound starlet is sleeping with what hot, young president? And who else is she sleeping with that he doesn't know about? Ma even knows whom she's going to sleep with next, which only her agent knows about.

How do they get such great gossip? Hey, they're the phone company. If they can't listen in, who can?

To sign up, just dial 1-800-Say-What.

•••

15. Inner football

Football: It's not just a game. It's spending the kids' inheritance for a bad seat to watch guys you hate get beaten up by other guys you would hate if you knew them better.

But don't think of season tickets as a stupid investment in idle worship. Think of it as a stupid investment in therapy.

You could spend $150 an hour to have some scruffy chin who couldn't crush a beer can on his forehead tell you you're all screwed up. Wasted money. You already know that.

Your team knows it too. That's why they soak you for the rights to be double-soaked for season tickets, even though they haven't won a Super Bowl in twenty-five years and aren't planning to.

Why should they go to all that effort to win when they can get rich by losing?

That's why they cram you into seats too small for your butt, then stuff you with Polish sausages and beer so that the seats get tighter as your butt swells each exciting week of the season.

That's why every player on the team has been convicted of aggravated assault. And guess what? Not one of them has ever served a day in prison. Why? Because they're football players, you dope. Society needs them. But it doesn't need you.

That's why they always seat a fat slob right behind you who spills beer down your back and busts your ear drums with a stupid horn that scientific studies have proven has absolutely no effect on the outcome of the game.

All this and less for only eighty-five dollars for a three-hour session. Plus $17.50 luxury tax, $8.50 to park in a muddy field, and a seventeen-cent charity surcharge.

No matter how much they soak you, it's still cheaper than psychoanalysis. And the results are the same: You get to vent. Plus, if you sign up now, they'll let you throw things at the players. That's why they wear helmets. If you hurt one, don't worry. There's always more where they came from.

Football: America's game. The Gestalt-Lombardian Interpersonal Therapy is free.

•••

16. Sweet-smelling knuckleheads

Plenty of products try to express a smart lifestyle. But is there anything besides Slurpees and Gap clothes designed for the dumb lifestyle?

Yes, they're just starting to market dumb products now.

For example, there's Ennui, the fragrance that reflects your lifestyle. Sort of.

At last you can smell the way you really feel. With Ennui, the fragrance that's hard to describe. Or put on. Or care about.

Ennui. Perfume for a man. Or a woman. Or whatever.

Every half-full, half-empty bottle of Ennui comes with a self-squirting applicator. Because the way you feel, who can be bothered?

With each purchase of fifty dollars' worth or more, you get absolutely nothing, absolutely free. Because that's the way life really is.

•••

17. Industrial boo-boos

You've seen signs like this at manufacturing plants: "Another forty-seven minutes without a serious industrial accident." But are industrial accidents a sign of worker stupidity or the result of management planning?

Neither. They're arranged by an outfit little known outside executive circles called Industrial Magic. Here's what their brochure offers:

> Industrial Magic: Because accidents happen. Don't they?
>
> Corporate layoffs? Downsizing? Firing the bums? Who are you kidding? Let's face it: The old way to get rid of workers you don't want anymore is cruel, humiliating, and dangerous.
>
> We have a new way: industrial accidents. Because the worker who dies on the job won't be coming back the next day with an Uzi looking for a manager.
>
> Put Industrial Magic to work for you. Whether it's a supervisor who's too highly paid. Or a plant full of

beer-guzzlers who don't know how to shut up and work overtime for free like the Chinese. Our industrial experts will arrange the perfect accident that will down-size your corporation without the fuss, the guilt, or the severance package.

One phone call will get us started. Ring twice, ask for Pete. Industrial accidents: the new way to say goodbye to old problems.

Be sure to ask your Industrial Magic agent about our new retirement fund. We're planning the future. You're not in it.

•••

18. The final diet

If you just want to tell people you're on a diet, then any diet plan will work. But if you actually want to lose weight and keep it off, then there's only one plan for you: the Ethiopian Diet.

In just four easy steps you will accomplish 25 percent more than you can in three easy steps.

Step 1: We take all your money and leave you in total poverty.

Step 2: You live on surplus food charity just like those svelte Ethiopians.

Step 3: We hire armed thugs to steal your surplus food scrap and resell it to us.

Step 4: Right before you die, you'll never have looked thinner.

19. Out-dancing depression

America seemed to be moving forward. Then it didn't. Then it kind of did. Now, who can tell? So youth wants to know: Is there a dumb way to get America moving forward again?

No, but we can get America moving from side to side.

Let's make every other Thursday National Dance Day. You'll feel a whole lot better and we'll get America back on its feet.

Here's an upbeat dance song to get the party started, number forty-five with a bullet from Shady Lady and the Pitz, "Everything Is Like a Prozac Delirium Except When I Got My Da-Da-Dancing Shoes On."

> Life stinks. War kills.
> No one thinks. Nothing thrills . . .
> So let's dance. Boogy-da-boogy. Let's dance.
> God's dead. Hope's gone.
> Stale bread. Elton John.
> So let's dance. Boogy-da-boogy. Let's really dance.

●●●

20. Better death

If life is so dumb, what's our alternative?

Death. It's the only time that the idiot and the genius have the exact same chance of success.

Life? Been there. Done that. So maybe it's time to cast off your old tired life and get ready for something new and exciting.

Well, new anyway. Death, the only game in town where everyone can play. No experience necessary. No rules. No dress code. Come as you are.

In the game of death, everyone's a winner. But you can't play if you don't die.

Death: the ultimate thrill ride.

●●●

21. The tax lottery

We've seen plenty of dumb attempts to fix our tax system, even though no government system can be fixed. It can only be broken in a different way.

But the IRS could make paying taxes popular by taking a tip from the lottery.

To pay your taxes, you'd file an IRS scratch card, Form 1040SC-RA-TCH. Then on April 15, the weatherman with the slickest hair would draw the winning numbers from the IRS drum. One tax player in ten million wins the IRS lottery and goes tax free for life.

Of course, that wouldn't help the IRS get rich people to pay their taxes. But free drinks handed out by IRS agents in rhinestone-studded G-strings should take care of that problem. Hey, it works for Vegas.

CHAPTER TWENTY-EIGHT

Stupidity by the Numbers

Eight Stupid Signs from Around the Globe

1. On a Burmese river road: "When this sign is under water, this road is impassable."
2. In a Nairobi restaurant: "Customers who find our waitresses rude should see the manager."
3. In an Indian maternity ward: "No children allowed."
4. At the Budapest Zoo: "Please do not feed the animals. Give all food to the guard on duty."
5. On a restroom hand dryer along an American turnpike: "Do not turn on machine with wet hands."

6. In a German cemetery: "Do not pick flowers from any but your own grave."

7. In a Parisian hotel elevator: "Please leave your values at the front desk."

8. At a dry cleaners in Rome: "Leave your clothes here and spend the afternoon having a good time."

●●●

Two Spectator Sports That
Could Easily Be Made Less Dumb

1. Hockey wouldn't be such a dumb sport if they just got rid of the puck.

    Then we wouldn't be distracted from watching big lugs hit each other with sticks. They could get rid of the ice skates too while they're at it.

2. *The Nutcracker* wouldn't seem like such a dumb ballet if the rats won every now and then.

●●●

Three Dumb Questions We Have No Answers To

1. If doctors and lawyers work in professional buildings, who works in amateur buildings?

2. Why do they always run us around in circles? Couldn't they run us in ovals or rectangles or figure 8s for a change?

3. Why are those ants always bragging they can lift thirty-two times their own weight? Big deal. I can lift thirty-two times their weight too. With one hand.

Three Dumb Theories of Creation

1. Human beings were one of God's early models. Now that God's off creating other races, He's worked out most of the bugs.

2. A superior race from another galaxy dumped us here, then ran away and has been hiding from us ever since.

3. It took more than one god to create this big a mess. Picture two gods hanging out at the Cosmic Café knocking back a few.

BIG JOE GOD: People, they'll believe anything.

FRANK "GOODIE" GOD: You think yours are gullible. I told mine that I created them because I loved them.

BIG JOE: And they believed you?

GOODIE: They've got no sense of humor. I mean, after all the earthquakes, fires, hurricanes, accidents in the shower, plus the itching, they still think I'm setting up some kind of Club Med for them after they're through down there.

BIG JOE: Pathetic, isn't it? They'll swallow any story that makes them feel like they've got a shot. Why don't we create something a little smarter next time?

GOODIE: Yeah, but let's have another round first.

•••

Three Ideas So Dumb They're Brilliant

1. Mood rings for cars.

   Every time you squeeze the steering wheel, lights indicate your mood to other drivers.

Watch out for that road-rage Volvo with the red light coming up on your left.

You see that T-Bird cruising the drag? Look at her amber light; she's just teasing.

2. All-loaner used car lot.

Have you ever put your own heap into a shop and had any problems with the loaner? Mechanics keep loaners in top shape because they're advertising their mechanical skills.

Plus, people don't trash loaners as they do rental cars. Everyone sends karmic signals back to the mechanics: If I take care of your car, give me a break and take care of mine.

3. Height-sensitive movie theaters.

Before you get in to see the movie, everyone lines up in order of height, short to tall, so you'll always be sitting behind someone you can see over.

Hey, it works in grade school. It'll work at the movies.

•••

Three Goofy Ideas That Used to Be Smart but Boy, Do They Sound Dumb Now

1. Go West, young man.

Two letters: LA.

If Horatio Alger had only said, "Go Midwest, young man," you'd still be able to park in Hollywood and get from the Valley to Malibu in under five hours.

2. A fool and his money are soon parted.

If he's such a fool, how did he get the money in the first place?

And if he and his money are soon parted, how come they weren't parted sooner than when they are parted? Why were they waiting for you to come along?

More accurately: A fool and his money are soon partied.

3. This country is going to hell in a handbasket.

Who carries a handbasket these days? What the hell is a handbasket anyway? As opposed to a footbasket or a fannybasket?

Why would you carry your stuff around in a basket when you can choose from a wide range of handbags, purses, fanny packs, backpacks, and multitasking omnipacks?

So relax, this country isn't going to hell in a handbasket. Clearly, we're going to hell in an SUV. It's so much faster that way.

●●●

Three Things You Should
Never Say to an Idiot

1. What makes you think so?
2. Would you like to hold my collection of crystal antiques?
3. Welcome, come on in.

●●●

Three Things You Hope You
Never *Have* to Say to an Idiot

1. Sure thing, boss.
2. Yes, dear.
3. Can you clarify that, Mr. President?

Three Things That Mean Big Trouble
If You Have to Say Them to an Idiot

1. But Your Honor . . .
2. Are you sure you have to operate, Doc?
3. You want us to charge which hill, General?

●●●

Three Businesses Only an Idiot Would Run

1. Day Two, a restaurant that serves only leftovers.
2. The Double Bill, a theater that shows two movies at the same time, so if you get bored with one you can watch the other.

Here's the schedule for the split screen:

Gone with the Wind and the Lion
A Few Good Men Don't Leave
The Man Who Would Be King Kong
My Favorite Year of Living Dangerously
Dead Man Walking Tall
Bob and Carol and Ted and Alice in Wonderland
The Good, the Bad and the Ugly American
The Princess Bride of Frankenstein
The Thin Man on the Flying Trapeze
Working Girl, Interrupted
The Russians Are Coming, the Russians Are Coming Home
Blue Steel Magnolias
Odd Man Out of Africa
Nine to Five Easy Pieces
Bob and Carol and Ted and Alice's Restaurant

Shakespeare in Love with the Proper Stranger
A Man and a Woman for All Seasons
The Maltese Falcon and the Snowman

3. Rent-a-Lemon Car Rental: Doesn't matter how much you beat up these junkers. Even we don't want them back.

•••

Three Rejections of Greatness
by Fools Who Couldn't See It

1. Ignace Paderewski was told his hands were too small to play the piano. He became one of the greatest pianists of all time.
2. When engineer Guglielmo Marconi developed his theory of radio transmission, the scientific authorities of his day dismissed the notion, explaining that his ideas ran contrary to the laws of physics.
3. Enrico Caruso was told to abandon opera because his voice sounded like "wind whistling through a window." He kept whistling in the wind and became the greatest operatic tenor of his time.

•••

Two Dumb Blonde Jokes
Versus Two Dumb Men Jokes:

1. The dumb millionaire is driving the wrong way down a one-way street. A cop pulls him over and asks, "Where do you think you're going?"

   "I don't know," the millionaire replies. "But I must be late because everyone else is coming back."

2. What do you call a man with half a brain?
    Gifted.
3. Why do psychiatrists charge blondes half price?
    They only have half a brain to analyze.
4. Why do blondes get only half an hour for lunch?
    So their bosses won't have to retrain them.

Actually, I reversed them. The first two jokes were originally dumb blonde jokes. Numbers 3 and 4 were originally dumb men jokes. But they work just as well the other way around, don't they?

●●●

Four Dumb Jobs

1. Actor
    Movie director Alfred Hitchcock disliked actors because they were hard to manage. Here's the great manipulator dreaming of the perfect actors: "Disney, of course, has the best casting. If he doesn't like an actor, he just tears him up."
2. Newspaper editor
    "An editor should have a pimp for a brother," writer Gene Fowler suggested, "so he'd have someone to look up to."
3. Lawyer
    "Lawyers are the only persons in whom ignorance of the law is not punished." Which attorney basher said that? The attorney Jeremy Bentham.
4. Politician
    "Being in politics is like being a football coach," Senator Eugene McCarthy said. "You have to be smart enough to understand the game, and dumb enough to think it's important."

Six of the Dumbest Things
the Human Race Has Ever Done

1. Create cities.

   Monstrously overcrowded cities are not even a modern invention. Constantinople, capital of the Byzantine Empire, was home to over a million people as early as the ninth century.

   But not happily. Hundreds of thousands of poor people were drawn to the city, thinking it had to be better than life in their miserable villages.

   They lived in the city's slums in such abject misery and squalor that their major hobby became rioting. Persecution of the poor became a prime city function, like sweeping the streets.

   Is this any way to live? Apparently so, since it's still done that way in mammoth cities all over the world.

   What if there were no huge cities? Then no sieges, no traffic jams, no plagues, thin walls, or dumb neighbors.

   You wouldn't have panhandlers on every corner if there weren't so many corners.

   No cities, no organized crime. No streets, no street gangs.

   Madness due to the stresses of overpopulation? Gone. Man goes mad on a mountaintop, who knows? Man goes mad downtown, he upsets the office staff on their way to lunch, requires police intervention, inspires other madmen to let loose.

   No cities, no ennui. Out in survival land, people are too busy to be bored.

   So what do cities give us in exchange for all that numskull

misery? A few good museums, some great restaurants, more hills to be king of.

Plus, better chances for plain guys to find good-looking girlfriends. It's a numbers game, and cities give you numbers.

2. The ten commandments.

Not complaining about the value system. All good. But too many of them.

Who are the top ten home-run kings of all time? The ten biggest box office hits? People can't remember ten of anything.

"Was that 'don't covet my neighbor's ox'? Or my neighbor's ass?"

God would have gotten a much better return on his moral investment if he had condensed. One good commandment would have done the job, and we'd all remember it: Thou shalt not be such a jerk.

3. The power behind the throne.

The king's not that big a problem. Everyone knows how to fool tough guys. Make them ruler of all they survey. That tends to keep them mollified. Your biggest challenge is making sure they don't survey too much.

But the powers behind the throne never stop meddling. They want more because they know that over the hill in the next tough guy's land, the powers behind that throne are just like them: They want more.

These guys are always buzzing in the king's ear: See those other guys over there? We'd better wipe them out before they wipe us out.

If there were no powers behind the throne, there would be no throne.

4. Short skirts. Long skirts. Makeup. Fashion.

How many centuries of women-hours have been wasted trying to look a little better for a little while?

If women took all that time they spend putting on and taking off makeup and shopping and studying what fashion is going to do to them next, and devoted that energy to fixing all the dumb things men have done to screw up the world, we wouldn't be in such a mess today.

5. Synonyms.

The English language means too many things. If we had fewer words, we'd lead smarter, happier lives with less stress.

Right now, we not only have stress. We have tension, pressure, anxiety, apprehension, trepidation, misgivings, and disquietude.

Life would be easier if we only had stress.

But English is designed to drive us all mad, in case the rest of the world isn't up to the job.

Your boss says, "Jones, you idiot," and you don't know where you stand. Sounds bad, but is it?

"Jones, you idiot" could still be a rung up from "That moron Smith in accounting." Or not.

Synonyms make people who know a lot of words feel superior, and that makes people who don't know as many words feel like punching them in the nose. Which leads to a lot more stress for everyone.

6. To-do lists.

Before to-do lists, we did the minimum we could get away with. If some task was really important, it didn't have to be remembered. It had to be *done*.

The operational rule: If whoever was in charge of nagging forgot about it, then you didn't have to do it.

Until the to-do list came along. To-do lists gave us obligations and guilt. Made it much less convenient to forget.

Now we preplan our planning meetings. But only after we prioritize the agenda for our preplanning session.

We keep lists that track our other lists.

We buy special pads of paper just for lists. When we run out, we write down on another list: "Buy new list pads."

Is there a way to break the terrible list habit? Sure, everything beyond number seven on any list—throw it away. It's not that important or it would work its way into the top five.

You ever wonder what the to-do lists of famous people were like?

Moses' To-Do List

1. Meet with Pharaoh.
2. Buy locust insurance first. *Then* meet with Pharaoh.
3. Figure out a good route to the promised land *before* leading that bunch of whiners into the desert.
4. When you go up the mountain to get God's commandments, take wheelbarrow. Stone tablets are heavy and there's no telling how many rules God will come up with once He gets started.
5. While up there, see if God has any ideas for something new to eat. People getting tired of matzo, matzo, matzo.

THEODORE ROOSEVELT'S TO-DO LIST

1. Go hunting tomorrow.
2. If press hangs around, remember to find an animal and set it free. Maybe they'll name it after me. Teddy rabbit sounds good. Maybe Teddy deer.
3. Avoid bears at all costs.
4. Consider whether motto should be "Walk swiftly and carry a small stick" or "Walk safely and carry a medium-size stick." Can't decide.

●●●

Four Areas Where Foolish
Spell Checkers Are Taking Over

Since only a few third graders can still spell, we let our computer's spell-checker make decisions for us, thereby correcting things we didn't even know needed correcting.

1. Rock bands

If it were up to our spell-checker, Mötley Crüe would be changed to Motley Crude.

The Doobie Brothers: The Doughboy Brothers

Simon and Garfunkel: Simian and Garfunkel

Lovin' Spoonful: Loin Spoonful

The Byrds: The Birdies

The Allman Brothers Band: The Alumna Brothers Band

Kool and the Gang: Koala and the Gang

Manfred Mann: Mannered Man

The Isley Brothers: The Islet Brothers

Emerson, Lake and Palmer: Emerson, Lake and Paler

2. Movies

Butch Cassidy and the Sundance Kid: Butt Cased and the Sundance Kid

Shrek: Shrike

Forrest Gump: Forrest Ump

Ben-Hur: Ben-Hurry

Unforgiven: Unforgotten

Rambo: Mambo

Stalag 17: Stag 17

Superfly: Superbly

Tora! Tora! Tora!: Torn! Toro! Torero!

The Guns of Navarone: The Guns of Nazarene

Mr. Blandings Builds His Dream House: Mr. Blandness Builds His Dream House

3. Books

The Hunchback of Notre Dame: The Hunchback of North Dame

Anna Karenina: Anna Keratin

Jane Eyre: Jane Eye

Barry Lyndon: Barry London

Les Misérables: Lease Miserable

The Picture of Dorian Gray: The Picture of Doorman Gray

Wuthering Heights: Withering Heights

4. Pop culture favorites

Betty Boop: Betty Oop

Tinkerbell: Thinkable

Godzilla: Good Will

Two Dumb Future Trends

1. Combo books.

     To increase our lagging productivity in reading, publishers will combine books. We can double our reading through-put with combo books like these:

> *Lake Wobegon Days of the Locust*
> *The Old Man in the Gray Flannel Suit and the Sea*
> *Romeo and Juliet and Franny and Zooey*
> *101 Dalmatians Flew Over the Cuckoo's Nest*
> *The Petrified Forrest Gump*
> *Tender Is the Night of the Iguana*
> *The Wings of the Lonesome Dove*
> *The Maltese Falcon and the Snowman*

2. Movie marketing, phase II: Beyond product placement.

     Hollywood will realize vast new fortunes (which they can stack on top of their vast old fortunes) when they take product placement off the screen and into the stores. Movies will go retail with products like:

Gone with the Windex: Tomorrow will be another dirty day. That's why down in the South we keep our vision clear with a window cleaner that frankly doesn't give a damn about dirt.

A Bug's Life Spray: The only bug spray that makes insects so darn cute, you'll treat them as guests, not pests.

Tootsie Rolls: The candy bar for people who are questioning their sexual orientation. Open at either end.

It's a Wonderful Life Insurance Company: You're in safe hands with Jimmy Stewart.

Malcolm X-ray Labs: We see into your body . . . and through their lies.

Who Framed Roger Rabbit Picture Frames: Your pictures aren't bad. They're just framed that way.

Thelma and Louise Dating Service: If you can catch them, you can date them.

The Dirty Dozen: Eggs the way nature intended them.

●●●

Five Signs That Our Legal System Wouldn't Be Much Wackier If It Had Been Created by Goo-goo Heads

When you think about our laws, they don't have to make sense. What's legal and illegal in our society is often just prejudice.

1 Using a sexy woman to sell everything from beer to autos: legal.

Using a sexy woman to sell sex: illegal.

2. Having sex with someone you just met in a bar and probably will never see again, then giving her fifty dollars for tickets to a church raffle: legal.

Having sex with someone you just met in a bar and probably will never see again, then giving her fifty dollars without the raffle tickets: illegal.

3. Taking drugs that make you want to hit the guy next to you with a barstool: legal.

   Taking drugs that make you want to hug the guy next to you in a drum circle: illegal.
4. Killing hundreds of people if the president says it's okay: legal.

   Killing one person without the president's okay: illegal.
5. Strong guy beats up weaker guy: illegal.

   Strong guy puts on gloves and beats up weaker guy: not only legal, but you can sell tickets to it.

●●●

Three Dumb Rules for Pilots

1. It's better to be down here wishing you were up there than up there wishing you were down here.
2. The propeller is a big fan in the front of the plane that keeps the pilot cool. Every time it stops, the pilot breaks out in a sweat.
3. Don't drop the aircraft in order to fly the microphone.

●●●

Three More Dumb Rules for Pilots

1. Flying is the second greatest thrill. Landing is the first.
2. Learn from others' mistakes. You won't live long enough to make them all yourself.
3. Don't forget the difference between God and a pilot. God doesn't think He's a pilot.

Four Examples of
Our Dumb Language

No matter how highly educated we are, most of us end up uttering silly phrases like these:

1. "Without further ado . . ."

    That's so unfair. It means you've already had your ado, but I don't get mine. The time to undo ados is before you get to the further part.

    But no one ever offers: "With ado, I'd like to introduce a guy who needs no introduction . . . the guy who popularized use of the salad fork and is well liked by many of his cousins. . . ."

    Hey, the only guy who needs no introduction is Jesus. Everyone else can use as much ado as they can get. Otherwise, why would there be someone figuring out where the ado cutoff line should be?

2. Premature ejaculation.

    Has any woman ever said, "Oh, Harold, that was such a mature ejaculation"?

    What if she says, "Sorry, too late." Does that make it postmature?

3. "That's like comparing apples and oranges."

    Why can't apples and oranges ever get along? They have so much in common: We eat both of them. They're fruit. You can juice either one. They're more or less round. They're good for you. They appear in the same sentence more than any other fruits.

    Not so hard to compare them after all, is it?

4. "Don't count your chickens before they hatch."

Really? Have you ever tried to count them after they hatch? They're all over the place. You're chasing one, missing four.

Then you think: All right, I'll hire a few chicken counters to help out. But how can you know how many chicken counters you'll need unless you count them before they hatch?

In fact, eggs turn out to cause endless problems. We say, "Don't put all your eggs in one basket."

What are you, like, made of baskets?

Let's say you've got a dozen eggs. If you put one in one basket, then the other eleven in another basket—you're still putting all your eggs (all eleven of them) in one basket.

Eventually, you'll need an infinite number of baskets for an infinite number of eggs, one in each. Then where are you going to put all those baskets? In a bigger basket!

"You can't make an omelet without breaking a few eggs."

Seemingly so incontrovertible, leaving aside the U.S. Army. But that egg-breaking crack completely misses the point of modern life: So few of us can make an omelet even *after* breaking eggs.

What can we do about it except switch to oatmeal? Nobody counts oats, and they don't hatch. You don't have to put them in baskets, and you couldn't break them if you wanted to.

Five Everyday Things
We Couldn't Get Right

1. If your house has two bathrooms, odds are one of them does not contain a bath.
2. In the kitchen we put cups in the cupboard. But we don't put plates in the plateboard.
3. We call them glove compartments, although no one keeps gloves in them.
4. Parkways don't lead to parks.
5. We eat eggplants without eggs, hamburgers without ham, and pineapples that have neither pines nor apples. We also pick at sweetmeats, which are meatless candies; and sweetbreads, which are unsweetened, breadless meat.

●●●

Six Signs That the Inhabitants
of Our Daily Comic Strips Are Dumber
Than the Inhabitants of Anywhere Else

A quick look at idiots who have been gainfully employed in comic strips gives us:

1. The lead character in *Hagar the Horrible*, *The Born Loser*, and *Andy Capp* (and Andy's wife is not too bright either).
2. Lieutenant Fuzz in *Beetle Bailey*, Jon in *Garfield*, Jonathan the brokerage-house boss in *Bulls 'n' Bears*, Artie in *Geech* (and maybe Merle), a tie between Brad and Tiffany in *Luann*, Moondog in *Monty*, Sluggo in *Nancy*, the pig in *Pearls Before Swine*, Royboy in *Soup to Nutz*, and the king in *Wizard of Id*.

3. In a few strips, just about everybody is an idiot; for example, *Li'l Abner*, *Charlie*, and *Dilbert*.

4. You'll find dumb dads starring in *The Buckets*, *Big Nate*, *Betty*, and *Rose Is Rose*.

   The dad in *Drabble* is saved from the list because his son, Norman, dumb-trumps everyone else.

5. Two of the most popular strips of all time present interesting challenges on the Stupid-O-Meter.

   Peanuts is too kid-kind to have a real idiot. But Marcie and Sally are mostly clueless. The free-spirited Snoopy is often out of touch with the world, but that may be a sign of his intelligence, not his stupidity.

   Doonesbury is populated with a variety of conditional idiots.

   Duke is sporadically stupid, depending upon the pharmaceuticals involved.

   Roland the reporter says stupid things all the time, but he is occupationally stupid because he works for TV news.

   Boopsie is one of the few dumb women working in comics, but her feeblemindedness never slows her down.

   Zipper is an interesting second-generation airhead, as blissed out as Uncle Zonker but with a diluted injection of Zonker's magic.

6. One of the best strips of all time had no idiots at all: *Calvin and Hobbes*.

The ingeniously diabolical little boy and his stuffed tiger are something rarely seen in comic strips: two best friends who together take on the world.

Bill Watterson, the genius behind the strip, chose not to take the obvious route and make the parents idiots. Calvin may sometimes get the best of them, but you can see where the boy inherited his stubborn deviousness.

It's interesting to see whom Watterson often casts in the role of the strip's idiot.

Take the panel where Calvin mourns the death (there's something you rarely see in comic strips) of a baby raccoon he found in the woods and (with the help of those non-idiot parents) tried to save.

"I didn't even know he existed a few days ago and now he's gone forever," Calvin laments. "It's like I found him for no reason."

A true friend, Hobbes has little consolation except his steady presence at Calvin's side.

"Still in a sad, awful, terrible way, I'm happy I met him," Calvin realizes, then hits the kicker: "What a stupid world."

Watterson knows that the world will take care of the idiocy for you.

One Warning Sign That
America's Getting Dumber

There are students who enroll at the Dunkin' Donuts Training School and then don't pass. Yes, America now has people too stupid to work in a doughnut shop.

CHAPTER TWENTY-NINE

What's the Dumbest Thing You've Ever Done?

Eighteen True Stupid Stories from Real People Just Like You, Except They're in the Book and You're Not

1. From winery owner June Smith

After enrolling my husband Jim in the national Jim Smith Society, we went to the convention in Washington, D.C., and left the name of the hotel with our business partner.

But when he needed to reach us, he had a terrible time, because everyone in the hotel was named Jim Smith!

•••

2. From writer Ann Parker

When I was a kid I thought it might be interesting to see what happened when you lit a whole pack of matches at once. Wow, it was impressive.

The fire startled me so much that I dropped the matchbook into the trash can in my parents' bedroom. The tissues in the can immediately ignited.

Panicked, I grabbed the nearest thing to douse the fire—and sprayed my mom's perfume on the flames, which promptly shot up three feet.

I escaped from this mini-inferno amazingly well: no burns, the house didn't burn down, and my folks never found out. Thank goodness for metal trash cans and quick-burning tissues.

•••

3. From bookstore owner Aillee DeArmond

I have never done anything stupid. But when I was eighteen, my parents went to Europe, leaving their car in my care.

Three of us went to town to get cigarettes. As I turned off Pacific Avenue, the guy sitting next to me lit a cigarette. Then he tried to light one for me off his, but kept the lit cigarette in his mouth and the unlit one in his hand.

This guy is a real idiot, I thought. While I was marveling at his stupidity, I ran into a parked car, which smashed into another parked car, which then bumped the car parked behind it.

A four-car accident and I was the only driver. The message here is that it is better to be well lit when driving.

4. From food columnist Donna Maurillo

I hosted some official visitors from Italy, who were in our city on a cultural exchange. Despite my Italian heritage, my language skills are a bit spotty. But that didn't keep me from showing off.

When one of the visitors couldn't find his glasses, I told him in Italian that he was "a little forgetful."

His reaction was dead silence. Only later did I realize that I'd called him "a little testicle."

•••

5. From grief counselor Gabriel Constans

As a teenager I agreed to photograph some friends streaking naked (remember when that was a big thing?) through our local mall.

I didn't realize it was the same day the Boy Scout and Girl Scout troops were showing their projects in the mall. Some of the parents were *rather* upset.

•••

6. From professional volunteer Anne Butterfly

When I was a seat filler one year at the Academy Awards, I stepped into my gown moments before we were to take our places for the show.

But I was wearing four-inch heels and cut a twelve-inch slit up my leg and fell flat on my face. Then I found out we could wear any old comfortable shoes under our formal gowns because we wouldn't be seen on camera. Some of the seat fillers even wore athletic shoes.

7. From writer Jane Parks-McKay

"When I was a teenager, I fell for a guy who worked at the gas station near our home. My dad lent me his hot Ford Cougar, which I later commandeered permanently.

I felt the *only* way I could see this guy was to burn up a tank full of gas fast, then go visit him at the station.

Not once did it occur to me—even when my Dad asked about the high gas bills—to get a *little* gas and go in to the station more frequently!

I did go out with the guy, but ended up liking his brother instead.

•••

8. From librarian Chris Watson

After working at a school fundraiser, my son and I had our picture taken together. When the photo was dropped on my desk at work, I was shocked to discover how much my son, at seventeen, looked like me at forty-eight. I pointed out the likeness to everyone I met.

That night when I showed the photo to my son, he looked at me and frowned. "You're kidding, right?" he asked. "You know they pasted a copy of my head onto your face, right?"

Sure enough, when I looked closer, I saw my son's baseball hat, distinctive jaw and smiling eyes peeking at me from under my own mane of hair. How could I be so blind?

The answer is that mothers of teenage boys will take any opportunity to get closer to their sons.

The other answer is that there are none so blind as those who will not see. I guess my bifocals weren't working that day.

9. From newspaper reporter Brenda Moore

Many other people have done this too—only usually they're male. I asked a woman when her baby was due; and, of course, she wasn't pregnant.

The moment was made worse by the circumstance. I was having my annual OB-GYN checkup, flat on my back, feet in stirrups, the whole humiliating bit. Luckily she was the nurse, not the doc, so I was spared any physical harm.

•••

10. From TV reporter Benjamin Dover

When I was three years old, the world seemed like a simple place to figure out. For instance, anytime you saw a cord protruding from an appliance, you simply plugged it in the wall and the item would go. Blenders would blend and fans blow cool air.

One day I noticed an old electric extension cord in the trash that my parents had thrown away, and saw an opportunity to upgrade my tricycle to an electrically powered vehicle. It was so obvious! According to this three-year-old's logic, anything with a cord plugged into the wall became motorized.

I wrapped the two exposed ends of the extension cord around the metal frame of the tricycle and secured the cord with electrician's tape. Then with great anticipation, I plugged the end of the extension cord into the electrical outlet in the garage.

But instead of zipping around on my motorized trike, I was rudely educated about the perils of electricity. But the breakers kicked in and did their job, turning the juice off while I lay wincing on the cement floor of the garage.

11. From minister Becky Irelan

I couldn't drive a car when I became a pastor. I would ride my bike in town, but had to have folks in the church drive me around to visit the outlying farms.

One day I visited a farmhouse where the woman's husband was dying of a brain tumor. My driver that day was old Ann, accompanied as always by her dog, a Yorkshire terrier named Trinket.

I went in to pray with the man. Then the dog and I headed for the back door. Several steps ahead of my elderly driver, I turned into the kitchen and saw the *pile*. Without a second's hesitation, I grabbed a handful of Kleenex and scooped up the poop.

Then I stopped. What was I going to do with it?

I couldn't put it in the kitchen garbage; it would smell. I couldn't turn around and head for the bathroom; the ladies were right behind me.

So, hoping for a trash can in the yard, I stuffed it into my purse—just in time for my parishioners to catch me in the act. I had a very red face. We all had a very good laugh.

What did I learn from the poop-in-the-purse episode? I had only been trying to save my driver from a little embarrassment. While that may have been a noble intention, my efforts didn't succeed in making the dog poop disappear.

It was just one of those inconvenient reminders that we can't always fix everything for everybody. When we try, we end up looking pretty foolish.

For those who make a habit of taking on everyone else's piles of problems, listen up: The job opening for Savior has long since been sewed up.

•••

12. From medical sonographer Robin Cunningham

It was Easter break and we didn't have a hotel reservation in Zihuatanejo. But my husband Bill is an optimist. "We'll find a place," he said, "no worries."

Playa del Sol, the only hotel with a vacancy in that Mexican town, was worthy of a spread in *Architectural Digest*. But we were the kind of travelers who pored over *Latin America on $3 a Day*, so I knew the price would be way out of our league. But Bill said, "Let's go for it!"

They gave us a kitchenette, a sumptuous bedroom, and a bathroom nicer than my own home. A view of the ocean and right on the beach. I wanted to live there. This was the nicest hotel room I'd ever been in.

I was tired of carrying around all our papers, my camera, and traveler's checks. So I looked for a place to stash them before we took off for town. Under the mattress seemed so cliché and the freezer too obvious. So I alighted upon the brilliant idea of putting our papers, passports, tickets, and money in the bathroom trash can. I put some paper towels on top to hide them, and we took off.

Going to town turned out to be a wild night in a tequila bar with ex-pats and lunatics. We danced on the tables and ran around in the moonlight on the sand. The rest is lost for eternity, but when we got back I was clearheaded enough to check for my stash.

The wastebasket in the bathroom was empty. I shrieked. Bill ran in and started laughing. All our stuff had been carefully laid out on the countertop like little children put to bed.

We had never been in a hotel where they emptied your garbage mere hours after you arrived, so I did not anticipate that possibility. I was thrilled that I had not lost my valuables, but I felt like we had exposed our inexperience in a uniquely idiotic way.

When I opened my eyes the next morning, it was very bright in the room. Not only had we fallen asleep with the curtain wide open, but our room faced the *palapa* restaurant so the other guests dined in full view of our crumpled bodies for God knows how long that morning.

My first vision was of Bill's face, which appeared to be covered in dried blood. "Are you bleeding?" I asked.

He got a funny look on his face, and said, "Are you?" Bill ran his finger over my cheek and popped it in his mouth. "Chocolate!"

On the pillows were the mints we had fallen asleep on. "Jesus, they should have asked us for references before they let us in here!" Bill said. I couldn't believe the level of lameness we'd managed. And we had not even been there one whole day.

In the *palapa* the young bartender came over to our table and, in the most gentle way, said, "My wife cleans your room, and she is worried that you will lose your things if you put them in the garbage. *Por favor, no en la basura.* She wanted me to ask you not to do that anymore."

The sweet part of this story is that Arturo and Rosa looked out for us for the rest of the week. They showed us the safe in the office, where we left our valuables. We managed to eat mints every night instead of sleeping on them.

●●●

13. From psychologist Offra Gerstein

A couple I was counseling discussed the wife's affair and used the man's name repeatedly. Later in the session, I referred to the husband by the lover's name. Blush time.

●●●

14. From travel writer Karen Kefauver

In the days before 9/11, airport security was more lax, giving dumb travelers a greater opportunity to exercise stupid errors in judgment.

Traveling from San Francisco to my parents' home in Washington, D.C., at Thanksgiving was a stupid decision in the first place. Then we landed in Pittsburgh, where I had to transfer for a flight to Virginia's Dulles Airport, which was close to D.C.

When I boarded the second plane, I was irritated that some idiot was sitting in my assigned seat. I found another one. Then I found out that this plane was flying, not to Dulles, but to Washington's National Airport.

I begged to use a cell phone, contacted my stepmom, and told her I had gotten on the wrong plane. Meanwhile, my dad had miraculously recognized my luggage at Dulles, picked it up, and gone home. My stepmom dashed to National to collect her very embarrassed stepdaughter.

It was one of the dumbest mistakes I ever made. But since my parents so kindly remind me of it frequently, I have never repeated it.

•••

15. From actor Daniel Hughes

When I was seven, everyone thought Jason and I were best friends because our families were together so often. But I hated him.

Jason was a bully who outweighed me by fifty pounds and would break my toys, steal things from me, and take every opportunity to humiliate me in front of people.

On the Fourth of July, our families had a barbecue at my house. Jason "accidentally" broke the legs off one of my action figures and poured juice over my head.

I decided to play a trick on him. I climbed onto the roof of the garage toting a watermelon the size of my torso. I held the watermelon over my head and called to Jason.

When I saw the top of his head, I threw the melon as hard as I could. It hit him square on the head. The watermelon burst and I ducked out of sight, laughing my head off.

The next thing I heard was Jason's mother screaming in

horror. "Call an ambulance!" someone howled. I peeked over the edge of the roof and saw Jason laying face down in an awkward position, his arm twitching and watermelon everywhere.

I was certain I had killed him. I think everyone else was too. The ambulance took him away. Jason's father tried to have me arrested. I was not. Our families have never spoken since.

Jason did not die, although he was knocked out cold. He wore a neck brace for a few days and recovered quickly. I was grounded for the remainder of my life.

When I went back to school in the fall, everyone said I had tried to kill my best friend, and no one would play with me. My friends eventually warmed up to me, but the story that I tried to kill Jason followed me all through high school. Jason never looked me in the face again.

●●●

16. From book editor Marilyn Green

Faux Pas was the pet gerbil in my sorority house at Michigan State. I took Faux Pas home for the Christmas holidays and my dog ate him . . . all but the tail.

Thinking that all gerbils look alike, we went to the pet store and bought another one. Turns out all gerbils may look alike, but not all gerbils know how to swim.

Faux Pas's caretaker came to me, hands on hips. "Marilyn, what happened to Faux Pas?"

"What do you mean?" I replied. I never let on.

17. From actor Bruce Burns

I was doing *Oliver!* and choreographed one of the dances. The actress and I doing the dance had an Astaire–Rodgers kind of move where we moved past each other, then grabbed and came back.

But one night, I couldn't remember if I was supposed to be upstage or downstage when I passed her. So my brilliant decision was to go for the middle.

Naturally, I knocked her down. I was mortified that I had forgotten my own dance. But in a dance number you can't stop. So I helped her up and we went on.

•••

18. From movie publicist Buff McKinley

The most ridiculous thing I've ever done was offer the following smug reply to a snotty flight attendant who said I couldn't sit with my friends on a crowded flight: "That's okay, we just won't tell you where we hid the bomb."

This was in the late 1970s and I was a smart-ass kid, with no idea that I was committing a federal offense. That fact was politely explained to me by the nice federal agent who met me at the gate in LA.

PART THREE

Looks Like We're
De-stupifying Again

CHAPTER THIRTY

How to Get Smarter by Cribbing from Actual Smart People

WHEN YOU put this book down and go back out into the world, you can be mostly smart or mostly stupid. I recommend mostly smart. Less competition.

To help you make the leap, here are some sharp tips from people who found a home in the world of the mentally unchallenged.

•••

1. Get started.

- Preacher Richard Evans: "Don't let life discourage you. Everyone who got where he is had to begin where he was."

- Thomas Edison: "Opportunity is missed by most people because it is dressed in overalls and looks like work."

- Henry David Thoreau: "If you have built castles in the air, your work need not be lost. That is where they should be. Now put foundations under them."

•••

2. Keep moving.

- Poet Henry Wadsworth Longfellow: "The lowest ebb is the turn of the tide."

- Writer John Hershey: "I have great contempt for intelligence all by itself. Coupled with energy and willingness, it'll go. Alone, it winds up riding the rails."

- Playwright George Bernard Shaw: "When I was a young man, I observed that nine out of ten things I did were failures. I didn't want to be a failure, so I did ten times more work."

- Car manufacturer Henry Ford: "Nothing is particularly hard if you divide it into small jobs."

- President Calvin Coolidge: "We cannot do everything at once. But we can do something at once."

•••

3. And when you're ready to quit, start moving again.

- Writer André Gide: "One doesn't discover new lands without consenting to lose sight of the shore for a very long time."

- Philosopher Ralph Waldo Emerson: "The hero is no braver than an ordinary man, but he is brave for five minutes longer."

- Violinist Fritz Kreisler (responding to a woman who had exclaimed, "I'd give my life to play as you do"): "Madame, I did."

- Minister Ralph Sockman: "Give the best that you have to the highest you know, and do it now."

•••

4. When they tell you it can't be done, you may be on to something.

- Inventor Charles Kettering: "The Wright Brothers flew right through the smoke screen of impossibility."

- Poet Struthers Burt: "Men are failures, not because they are stupid, but because they are not sufficiently impassioned."

- Greek historian Plutarch: "Many things which cannot be overcome when they are together, yield themselves up when taken little by little."

- Writer Samuel Butler: "Life is like playing a violin solo in public and learning the instrument as one goes on."

- Politician John Foster Dulles: "The measure of success is not whether you have a tough problem to deal with, but whether it's the same problem you had last year."

5. Follow a real leader, if you can find one.

- Businessman H. Gordon Selfridge: "The boss says, 'Go!' The leader says, 'Let's go!'"

- Therapist Paul Goodman: "Few great men could pass Personnel."

- Business magnate J. Ogden Armour: "Nothing will make more for loyalty and energy in an organization than the knowledge that employees are being promoted continually from the bottom. It gives men ambition, it gives them pride; and pride and ambition . . . will keep a man working at top speed when money is merely a by-product."

- Roman philosopher Lucius Seneca (to Emperor Nero): "However many you put to death, you will never kill your successor."

- Mount Holyoke College founder Mary Lyon: "Trust in God—and do something."

•••

6. Don't waste your time.

- Inventor Charles Kettering: "You will never stub your toe standing still. But the faster you go, the more chance you have of getting somewhere."

- Songwriter Noël Coward: "I write at high speed because boredom is bad for my health."

- Writer Samuel Johnson: "While you are considering which of two things you should teach your child first, another boy has learnt them both."

- English politician Lord Chesterfield: "Take care of the minutes for the hours will take care of themselves."

- Philosopher Ahad Ha-am: "Wise men weight the advantages of any course of action against its drawbacks, and move not an inch until they can see what the result of their action will be. But while they are deep in thought, the men with self-confidence come and see and conquer."

- General Electric chairman Owen D. Young: "Being slow and sure usually gets around to being just slow."

- History professor C. Northcote Parkinson: "During a period of exciting discovery or progress, there is no time to plan the perfect headquarters."

- Motivational speaker Dale Carnegie: "Ask yourself what is the worst that can happen. Then prepare to accept it. Then proceed to improve on the worst."

- English politician Sir Barnett Cocks: "A committee is a cul-de-sac down which ideas are lured and then quietly strangled."

- Business advisor Charles Brower: "The good ideas are all hammered out in agony by individuals, not spewed out by groups."

- Art historian Bernard Berenson: "Each day as I look, I wonder where my eyes were yesterday."

7. Copy the clever moves.

- English politician Lord Chesterfield: "Be wiser than other people if you can, but do not tell them so."

- Scientist Linus Pauling: "The best way to have a good idea is to have a lot of ideas."

- Writer Samuel Butler: "To do a great work, a man must be very idle as well as very industrious."

- Wanda Landowska (a master of the harpsichord): "I never practice. I always play."

- Businessman Robert Wieder: "Anyone can look for fashion in a boutique or history in a museum. The creative person looks for history in a hardware store and fashion in an airport."

- Writer A. H. Weiler: "Nothing is impossible for the man who doesn't have to do it himself."

- Business advisor Charles Brower: "There is no such thing as soft sell and hard sell. There is only smart sell and stupid sell."

- Newspaper publisher E. W. Scripps: "Never do anything today that you can put off till tomorrow . . . Most things that you do not have to do today are not worth doing at all."

- Historian Arnold Toynbee: "History not used is nothing, for all intellectual life is action, like practical life."

8. **Wisdom, courage, vision.**

- Baseball player Vernon Law: "Experience is a hard teacher because she gives the test first, the lesson afterwards."

- IBM president Thomas Watson Jr.: "I never hesitated to promote someone I didn't like. The comfortable assistant—the nice guy you like to go on fishing trips with—is a great pitfall. Instead, I looked for those sharp, scratchy, harsh, almost unpleasant guys who see and tell you about things as they really are. If you can get enough of them around you, and have patience enough to hear them out, there is no limit to where you can go."

- Minister Doug Larson: "Wisdom is the reward you get for a lifetime of listening when you'd have preferred to talk."

- Newspaper publisher E. W. Scripps: "When you find many people applauding you for what you do, and a few condemning, you can be certain that you are on the wrong course because you're doing the things that fools approve of. When the crowd ridicules and scorns you, you can at least know one thing, that it is at least possible that you are acting wisely."

- Book publisher Elbert Hubbard: "Every man is a damn fool for at least five minutes every day. Wisdom consists in not exceeding the limit."

- Lecturer and writer Helen Keller: "To know the thoughts and deeds that have marked man's progress is to feel the great heartthrobs of humanity through the centuries. And if one does not feel in these pulsations a heavenward striving, one must be deaf to the harmonies of life."

- Merchant J. C. Penney: "Courage is a quality which grows with use. It may take nerve to give up a position where you are doing fairly well and to take a lower one somewhere else. But if you have courage and ambition you can do it. The breaking away is the hardest part."

- Inventor Thomas Edison: "Genius? Nothing! Sticking to it is the genius! Any other bright-minded fellow can accomplish just as much if he will stick like hell . . . I failed my way to success."

- And finally, the John Wayne method of acting, straight from the Duke: "Talk low, talk slow, and don't say too much."

Works for a lot of other things too.

Bob Fenster is a writer living in Santa Cruz, California. He also tours with his one-man show, *The Stupid History of the Human Race.*